An Unexpected Joy

An Unexpected Joy

The gift

of parenting

a challenging child

Mary Sharp, M.D.

PIÑON PRESS ®

Piñon Press
P.O. Box 35007, Colorado Springs, CO 80935

ISBN 1-57683-461-1

Cover photo by Tim Platt/The Image Bank/Getty Images
Cover design by Dave Kottler/APEX Communications, Inc.
Creative Team: Terry Behimer, Karen Lee-Thorp, Cara Iverson, Kathy Mosier, Pat Miller

Some of the anecdotal illustrations in this book are true to life and are included with the permission of the persons involved. All other illustrations are composites of real situations, and any resemblance to people living or dead is coincidental.

Bible versions used for Scripture quotations include: the HOLY BIBLE: NEW INTERNATIONAL VERSION® (NIV®). Copyright © 1973, 1978, 1984 by International Bible Society. Used by permission of Zondervan Publishing House. All rights reserved; and the *King James Version* (KJV).

Sharp, Mary, MD.
  An unexpected joy : the gift of parenting a challenging
child / Mary Sharp.
     p. cm.
  Includes bibliographical references.
  ISBN 1-57683-461-1
  1. Javier, John Dominic Mahlon--Mental health. 2. Sharp, Mary, MD.
3. Autism in children--Patients--United States--Biography. 4.
Mothers--United States--Biography. 5. Caregivers--United
States--Biography. I. Title.
RJ506.A9J387 2003
618.92'8982--dc21
                                        2003008365

Printed in Canada

1 2 3 4 5 6 7 8 9 10 / 07 06 05 04 03

Contents

Thank-You's

*T*o say that I could have written this book without help would be hilarious. While I owe thank-you notes to a million people, I especially want to mention the following:

My literary midwives: Linda Peckham, Terry Behimer, and
Karen Lee-Thorp

My pastoral team: The Reverend Caroline Stacey and Doris
Strife

My prayer matrix:

Church girls—Pat, Renee, Kathy, Amy, Martha, and Pat

College girls—Karen, Cheryl, Donna, and Sara

Girl docs—Kathy, Julia, and Diane

Art girls—Bonney, Deidra, Nancy, Julie, and Jane

Good ol' girls—Jill, Jo, Alicia, and Susie

Angel babysitters—Melissa, Kitchie, Alicia, Gretchen, Steve,
and Neely

My beloved family: Rafael, Honora, Richard, and John
Dominic

Introduction

*"In the beginning God created the heaven and the
earth. And the earth was without form, and void;
and darkness was upon the face of the deep. And the
Spirit of God moved upon the face of the waters."*
(Genesis 1:1-2, KJV)

ll acts of creation come out of the chaotic primordial void.
In a child with autism, the chaos holds on for a little
longer.

I have come to regard my son Nic as the miracle God intended
him to be. He is physically beautiful. His tall, willowy body has a
spastic grace. He sits in postures reminiscent of Noel Coward or
Fred Astaire, his legs crossed and his hands folded. When he leaps
up in a burst of excitement and his energy flows down to his hands,
they start flapping back and forth so fast I wonder why he doesn't
become airborne. When he is excited about something, he often
squeals or shouts and then stops flapping. He rubs his hands
together so fast that I suspect if we could place a stick between those
hands, he could spark a fire. In those moments, his eyes shine.
When he was little and didn't talk, his brother said to me, "Momma,
he's talking with his eyes. Don't you see his eyes laughing?"

My spiritual growth has been intimately woven together with the development of this child. I have learned faith and patience beyond what I would have believed possible. I have slowed down enough to see God's works surrounding me, and I have been humbled. We have winnowed the chaff from the wheat and have reaped a rich harvest.

Here is our story. I pray to God it is helpful for you.

chapter
1
Our Family

*T*he isolation that families with a disabled child experience is hard to appreciate. Family and friends often don't understand, and their well-intended advice worsens the alienation. Dear friends tried to comfort me, but I experienced their words as patronizing platitudes that did not acknowledge the depth of the disturbance in my child and our household. It was just more confirmation that no one understood what we were dealing with and that we were out there on our own.

I think it would have helped me if I had found another mother who had been through this and didn't look shell-shocked. Or she could have looked shell-shocked if she could still speak. And laugh. I needed someone to tell me that even with all our unanswered and not-very-well answered questions, it would get better. Because it does get better—if you let it.

I hope I can be that recovering shell-shocked mother for you. Let me first take you back to that dream time before autism changed everything.

Third Time's a Charm

Life was good. Who could want for more? My new husband, Rafael, was handsome, kind, and smart. He was the kind of father many men aspire to be. He fell in love with me partly because of my toddler daughter, Honora. He loved to disappear into the toddler world after a tiring day in the adult world (he and I are both physicians). The depth of silliness Nora and Rafael were able to explore was a balm to his serious soul.

The birth of our first son, Rico, was much anticipated but surrounded by some tough events. At the end of the pregnancy I became ill with a bizarre form of arthritis, which basically put me in bed for about six months. It was associated with severe fatigue. My father first tried to commit suicide a week after Rico was born. He lay hovering in an ICU in Florida as I lay hovering on a couch in Michigan, trying to nurse our newborn son. Rico's emerging sense of humor was the only joy that permeated the fog. He smiled and giggled at about four weeks of age. He hasn't stopped laughing since.

After I healed from that illness and returned to work when Rico was seven months old, I started to see another baby in the picture. This surprised me. I subscribed to the zero population growth theories of my college peers of the early 1970s. Weren't two children enough? But I would look at the two little ones playing together. Nora mothered her little brother, making him laugh and smile. And I began to sense there was another baby out there intended for our house.

I began to crave this other baby. This was difficult to talk about because my husband didn't feel any need for another baby. He thought a girl and a boy, both healthy, were great. I also found it hard to talk about because I thought it was almost greedy. And it was hard to explain the highly irrational nature of this craving and vision. It was almost like this baby was a shadow playing with the other two.

I prayed a lot. Mostly it was, "God, please take this craving from me." The answer came back repeatedly: "There is nothing the matter with wanting to have another baby. This is not a sin." This repeated day after day, week after week, until it dawned on me that God wasn't going to budge on this answer. My faith has taught me that this is a pretty classic God practice. When ideas or themes keep reoccurring in one's internal conversations, there's a high likelihood that God may be trying to give you a message. No pleading, bargaining, or reasoning seemed to work. Finally, I just gave in. I cried when I told my husband about this struggle. Then I talked to his mother about it.

I always refer to my mother-in-law as a professional mother-in-law. She was really good at it. She thought I was swell and that my children walked on water. She never gave advice that wasn't asked for. She had seven children and had lived through the Japanese occupation of the Philippines in World War II. The Japanese had captured her husband; his brother carried him the last few days of the Bataan Death March while she was starving with five children in the caves outside of Baguio. My husband and his younger brother were born after the war. This lady had lived a lot, and her priorities were right on: family and bingo. Also, she had a rich prayer life, with daily recitation of the rosary right before she watched her soap operas. She was much loved. Grandchildren (including those in their twenties) regularly came to blows over who got to sleep with her when she came to visit.

Mamang (mother in Tagalog, my husband's Filipino dialect) did not feel that wanting another child was any issue at all. Rafael should comply with my wishes on the subject and consider himself lucky for having married someone who felt this way. He came home a few days later after having lunch with her, somewhat chastised, and said we could go ahead and try, but he didn't want me calling him up at the office and telling him to come home and get me pregnant. I didn't have another period after that; I was pregnant in two weeks.

I craved waffles that pregnancy. The kids got sick of bacon, which was the only protein I could stand to get near. Having been believers in the myth of control, we decided to have a chorionic villous sampling. Rafael took the day off from work, and we drove down to the specialist who was doing them in our area. The ultrasound technology was amazing to me. It had improved since Rico's time in utero. It was live, unlike those flat pictures they took of him. The definition was so good that it almost had a 3-D character to it. I fell in love with the sixteen-week life floating around inside me. It was the first time I cried for joy.

The pregnancy was unremarkable. I experienced the common pregnant woman practice of worry and bargaining with God. I prayed, "Please, I can handle anything you send me — cerebral palsy, missing limbs, dwarfism, bronchopulmonary dysplasia — anything but autism." The image of those silent, unfeeling specters I'd seen so infrequently in my life hung like a pall. I've talked to other mothers of autistic kids, and many of them tell me they knew something was up during their pregnancy. I felt good most of the time, but the summer was long and hot, and my fatigue was bad. I worked part time and was busy with two-year-old Rico and five-year-old Honora. We planned that I would take three months off before returning to work and we would engage an au pair. My friend with twins had been lucky enough to have an angel from Holland show up in her life for their first year, so we used the same agency. We did not get an angel.

The Au Pair from Hell

Karoline arrived from Holland two days before Nic would be delivered. She "loved children." *From what planet?* I later asked myself. Rico developed an immediate, intense dislike of her. He is an excellent judge of character, and I should have paid attention earlier. She was shocked when Rico gave her a hard time. She wore white overalls on their trip to the park and was dismayed when they ended up dirty. She was miserable and chose to console herself in food and American popular culture. She insinuated that I could not be a competent parent with my lack of knowledge about TV sitcom stars and the movie industry. Our grocery bill doubled; the turnaround time on the ice cream in the freezer was less than twenty-four hours.

She tried to carve out a niche by becoming the cook, but she could only cook spaghetti. My father nearly lost it the evening of the sweet corn. A high holy day for those of us in the Midwest is the day the sweet corn hits the roadside stands. We eat bushels of it. It is an exquisite pleasure, enhanced by sharing with loved ones. Four or five sticks of butter make it onto the table. The rest of the food is planned around the corn. It is a delicate decision: *What protein won't take up too much tummy space?* Tomatoes, for the color alone, are required. Fruit pie with ice cream may push the indiscrete over the edge. But to us seasoned eaters, none of it is too much. There is no place we would rather be than sitting around a table (preferably outside), wolfing down corn, chicken, tomatoes, and peach pie with those we love.

Enter Karoline. Bad vibes. You would have thought we asked her to sit down to eat a bale of straw. She became uncharacteristically quiet. She was like an ice cube. She stared at us with a shocked look. She grudgingly cleared plates after the worst of the frenzy. She spat out as she left the table, "In my country, this is pig food!" She wouldn't even try it. Too weird. We should have known she had a screw loose.

It went downhill from there. She left after being with us for one month. I developed a raging mastitis with horrible chills and eventually a fever of 104 degrees. I still remember when the lady from the agency came to get her and take her to a family in Kalamazoo. It was like a toxic energy element had been removed. We all breathed a sigh of relief. I thought things would start to settle down. It was easier to have a fever of 104 and three children—including an unbelievably colicky newborn—without her there than it had been with her boiling spaghetti and attempting to change Rico's diapers against his will.

Big Baby Boy Birth

Rico's birth had been precipitous, to say the least. It took only fifty minutes, start to finish. Dr. B. and I both thought it would be a good idea not to deliver Nic on the kitchen floor as my friend Mary Lou did with her last baby. We agreed that I'd come in a few days before my due date so he could induce my labor.

He ruptured my membranes at 10:00 A.M. A contraction started at 10:20 when no one was in the room with me. Nurses had gone off to check on other patients. Dr. B. was doing rounds. My folks, husband, and daughter had gone down to the cafeteria for coffee. They didn't want Honora to get bored. Rico, at two-and-a-half, was home with Karoline, giving her a hard time with changing his poopy diapers.

I was uncomfortable being alone, so after about ten minutes of this one contraction, I pushed the buzzer to get the nurse's attention. She strolled in, relaxed and calm, and asked if things had started up. She checked me and found me to be completely dilated and the baby starting to crown. She flipped into Keystone Kop mode and pushed what I thereafter thought of as "the panic button." This called in about five of her sister nurses, who all scrambled around, getting the bed set up, doing whatever prep they could do, and locating husband and doctor. Husband, in cafeteria, almost didn't answer his overhead page because he was off-duty, having his baby today. My mother suggested he answer it. He ran upstairs to my room while she waited for Honora to finish her cocoa. He arrived around the time the doctor did, who gently nudged my very competent nurse out of the way so he could catch the baby.

At 10:50 I pushed out Nic, an eight-pound, nine-ounce big baby boy. Each of my other two had been seven-and-a-half pounds. I remember feeling exhausted as they handed me this huge baby. I thought, *Oh, boy—he'll feed and sleep easy.* He looked like the Buddha. We named him John Dominic Mahlon Javier—after both grandfathers, plus a professional-sounding name in case he wanted to go into business.

| chapter 2 | *Life with Nic* |

*B*ut our visions of John Javier the businessman or Nic Javier the whatever soon melted into the day-to-day reality of living with Nic. For years we had no diagnosis, and then conflicting diagnoses, for his condition. He was seven-and-a-half years old when we finally received a definitive diagnosis of autism. Before this, all we knew for sure was that living with him was awful much of the time. He didn't sleep. His hypersensitivities revealed themselves over time in a multitude of ways. We seemed to have to figure everything out by ourselves.

He was touch averse and noise averse. He couldn't stand to wear tight clothes or many textures, so he would scream when wearing blue jeans, and I couldn't figure out what was making him miserable. Our attempts to physically soothe him usually made things worse. Loud noises often spooked him and made public places terrifying for him.

He was hungry all the time and threw up frequently. We could never figure out what would set him off. The more he threw up, the more he wanted to eat. The more he was overfed, the more he threw up. We had him evaluated by specialists for the vomiting. One of them misread a study and thereby delayed effective treatment for two years.

The hyperactivity was exhausting. Nic was "on" all the time. His favorite position when we were out in public was sitting on my shoulder, clinging to my neck. Sometimes I felt like I had a parrot instead of a child. He liked to climb on everything. Tall, expensive appliances were his specialty, but his interests also included bookshelves and cars. He was attracted to just about anything that was potentially dangerous.

He was temperature insensitive, so he would get frostbite and not know to come in from the cold. He burned himself on a steam radiator while I had my back turned for thirty seconds. Having these kinds of mishaps is normal for toddlers, but most eventually grow out of it. Nic continued for years.

He was also delayed in toilet training for a long time. We have cleaned up more poop than I can bear to think of. There is a huge difference between a one-year-old's poop and a seven-year-old's.

The tantrums were, and still are, the worst of it. He gets so frustrated that tantrums seem like his only option for expression. The tantrums can go on for hours, leaving the whole family in a quivering, raw heap of exhaustion. The slightest thing can precipitate them, like the Happy Meal coming in the wrong-colored bag or the cartoon show time getting switched. There is no logic system that works. It doesn't matter that we have no control over these events. No discipline techniques work because you can't reach the kid when his neurologic system flips into this mode. It has been like walking on eggshells for years. It's much better now, but it still happens, and afterward he is as mortified as we are exhausted.

For years the delays in development were heartbreaking. Nic's speech was profoundly delayed. Many autistic children develop lots of language, and Nic has developed beyond our expectations. Some children never develop speech, however, and to see Nic left in the dust as his same-age peers went on to develop normally was a persistent sorrow. When the dust settled and we had readjusted our expectations, the growth often seemed like a miracle. Gains our other children made with barely a smile from us were cause for celebration when Nic made them.

Anxiety and Dead Ends

Because autism is an invisible disability, the public feels free to make any kind of unsolicited judgment they feel necessary. They would never say this stuff to a family with a child in a wheelchair. I remember the cart operator in Florida who advised us that we needed to hit our child. I remember the manager in the armory lunchroom in Central Park: "You really must control that child!" *No, honey, I really like it when he screams like this.*

One of the definitions of *anxiety* is "a prolonged hypervigilant state." That is what life was like for years. Anxiety changed my personality. I lost my sense of humor. My little lifeboats started to float off, one by one. Like friendships, hobbies, and my relationship with my husband. We found that parental participation in any pleasurable activity, like sex or watching TV or going out to dinner, would precipitate a crisis that interrupted that activity. A life like this can turn a formerly high-functioning adult into a raw wreck of a parent.

I look back and see many times that we went down dead ends, but I figure we learned a tiny bit on each of those paths, so the efforts must have been for something. I ask God about that a lot.

Sometimes I get answers, and sometimes I don't. When I don't get an answer, I figure we were down that path for someone else's growth, not our own. God is not going to violate confidentiality by telling me how we helped someone else learn something. I think of all the medical personnel we've worked with over the years and I hope we contributed something to their understanding that made it better for those who came after us.

Adrift in an Epidemic

We looked for help in books. We read all kinds of things written by psychologists and other professionals that just didn't cut it. I read whole books in which the technical terms were so obscure that I never knew what the author was talking about. They tended to be calm, dry, and clinical. Token economies (used in many behavior modification programs) don't work if your child doesn't care about anything. Some of the social workers took whole books to state the obvious. Then they offered inane suggestions like, "Try and talk other kids into playing with your weird kid. It'll be good for both of them."

The parent-authored literature often felt like betrayal. None of those books spoke of the grief I was experiencing. Many of them gave brief synopses of their situations and then went on to "sell" me a cure. They offered "expert opinions" about phenomena in which they had had no formal education. They weren't helpful to me because they left out the emotional impact of what it is like to live with a child with so many problems. This worsened the sense of frustration and isolation for me. I feel strongly that I had to address my chronic grief, as painful as that was, before I could go on to make mature, responsible decisions for Nic.

The terms used by professionals are not uniform, and many professionals are caught up in diagnostic differentiation. This means they are more focused on what is going on than on how we are going to cope with it or optimize the outcome. This makes sense from a research and theoretical point of view but has little to do with where the rest of us live. The educators, speech pathologists, occupational therapists, psychiatrists, and medical doctors all use different languages. It makes me think of that parable about the blind men describing the elephant to each other. One has hold of the tail, another the ear, another the trunk. Surprisingly, having training in one of those exclusive languages didn't make it any easier for us. We believe it may have impaired our ability to get help.

Other terms used to describe this constellation of symptoms are Autism Spectrum Disorder, Asperger's Syndrome, Pervasive Developmental Disorder, and Pervasive Developmental Disorder Not Otherwise Specified (NOS). Many parents are extremely resistant to these diagnoses. I have seen patients resign themselves to the diagnosis of terminal lung cancer more easily than some parents adjust to a diagnosis of autism. I think this fear is part of the denial that is normal with the grief these parents are experiencing. Unfortunately, it contributes to an underestimation of the true number of affected individuals.

If you look at the growth of the population diagnosed with Autism Spectrum Disorders, we are in the midst of an epidemic. A spectrum disorder means that there are a variety of ways that a condition can present itself and that there is great variation in how individuals are affected. Some people with autism have no language and act like automatons. Some are so high functioning that they marry, hold down jobs, and can write books about their condition. When Nic was diagnosed, the literature quoted the incidence as four in ten thousand. Now the incidence is felt to be closer to one in five hundred. I have even read some articles that cite an incidence of one in two hundred fifty. This means that at least a million individuals in this country are affected with autism.

The Big Picture

Our public health system is so sabotaged by politicians' agendas and the American public has become so fond of "cause"-related funding that chronic problems, unglamorous as they are, fall to the back of the line. The media love to focus on physically dramatic health issues. Television shows about medicine usually tell stories about emergency room drama or surgical victories because they're so graphic. These dramatic cures are also quick and thus suitable for the public's limited attention span. The subtlety and nuance involved in managing the care of chronic disease is not glamorous or dramatic and so makes poor fodder for popular culture.

The medical system focuses on diagnosis. That's excellent for the appropriate treatment of cancer. But with chronic developmental disorders—those conditions associated with mental retardation—this approach is ludicrous. No one is coordinating treatment programs or comprehensively evaluating outcomes of kids with developmental disabilities. There is no standard treatment. Our society gives these children's health issues only token attention. In fact, we have demedicalized the developmental disorders and have dumped the responsibility for maximizing these kids' potential into the public school systems. This is good in some respects, bad in others.

The community groups, like the Autism Society, are blunted in their effectiveness for many reasons. They depend on volunteers from the exhausted and often terribly angry families they are trying to serve. I know families who just don't want to belong to that "club" because they're still in denial about their needs. All the developmental disabilities produce similar needs. The little subdiagnosis cliques that families get caught up in fragment the larger population that needs serving. This fragmentation also blunts our political effectiveness. If we had all the families of kids with Down's Syndrome, Pervasive Developmental Disorder, Asperger's Syndrome, Fragile X, Autism Spectrum Disorder—anything that produces retardation— united, we could be a significant political lobby. I think that sort of thing on a day when I'm frustrated by the larger society.

On an inwardly focused day, I think the social world we would construct for these kids would be more fun. The support network for families would be larger if we could get all these groups together who wish to serve disabled kids. The groups our school system has tried to support are stifled by regulation. Student confidentiality prevents you from getting a mailing list together. I fantasize about having a day at the movies for the developmentally disabled, where nobody would bat an eye at odd noises or peculiar motor activity. I'd like to go on a picnic, a fishing trip, or even a cruise with other families who understand and are tolerant of these behaviors.

If autism were infectious, like mad cow disease, it would be on the front page of every newspaper in the country. The long-term impact may be every bit as devastating. The need for long-term care for this population is going to be enormous. We are in the midst of massive cultural denial about a disorder affecting our youth in epidemic proportions.

As frustrated as I get when I see this big picture, I remind myself that even my capacity to see it is progress. Years ago, I had no energy to look further than today's tantrum or the next hour's attempt to sleep. I couldn't begin to grieve for a national epidemic when grief for my own family overwhelmed me. That was the first step, I came to realize: More than a book with brilliant diagnosis and treatment options, I needed to know how to grieve.

chapter
3 | *Grief*

The Amusement Park of Life

*I*n proper guru fashion, I say this to you in a calm tone, with my hands pressed together in prayer: "There are many rides in the amusement park of life." I've found it's rare to meet people who haven't been on any of the rides. Sometimes the ones I *do* meet are so sweet and innocent they are breathtaking. Sometimes they are so self-centered and insensitive they are breathtaking. Those who are profoundly insensitive may indeed have been on many of the rides, but they didn't know it. They were so busy looking at themselves that they missed the ride. I figure that problem is between them and God, and I tend to run in the other direction. It is very rare to run into an old person who hasn't dealt with something painful. Few get out of this world unscathed.

Some of the rides have things in common. Some have their own unique details. The "taking care of dying parents" ride has two basic variations. These are "Saints helped me get through this" or "The medical establishment completely abandoned me." Alcoholism and drug addiction are a whole little theme park unto themselves. Sexual abuse and rape are particularly large rides, with many terrifying twists and turns. Divorce is a very popular ride.

All of these rides disorient our true selves. When we survive these rides, we often feel exhilarated and really alive. After a ride, we stagger around on terra firma and try to get our balance. I've found it's not helpful to get back on another ride too soon, though I know people who for some reason just can't keep from getting back on.

When I've been in one of those in-between times, walking around the park, eating a corn dog and lemon freeze, I've found life can be pretty sweet. Sometimes I see people gorging on apache bread or cotton candy and I wonder if they're bored. It looks to me like they're killing time while waiting for the show. I want to shake them. This is the real thing! This is as good as it's going to get. Wake up!

Grief—and how we process it—is the mechanism of all these rides. Most medical schools discuss acute grief in a theoretical framework. Acute grief often contains elements of shock, extreme sadness, anger, self-recrimination, remorse, and loneliness that lead to deep isolation. If you are part of a community, after a tragic event, neighbors, friends, family, and religious community members gather around you when you're wounded. People show up at your door with casseroles. If there is a huge tragedy, like September 11, the nation, briefly, becomes one very large community. Acute grief gets processed, and if you are healthy, you move on to a new life—usually sadder, wiser, and more compassionate. If by two years you are not walking in shoes that feel like your own most of the time, it's medically called "pathologic grief." You can get help for that if you have the insight, energy, and money.

Prolonged grief is a form of hell. No one shows up with brownies. Because our grief was ongoing, Rafael and I found it hard to get resolution. The first part of our life with a child with severe disabilities was chronic, endless grief. We started to get resolution by really and truly letting die the image of the child we thought we had. We had to let a lot of dreams die. I found this a fertile place for God.

We had to let go of the future we had planned. The simple image of the family sitting around on a couch watching a video eluded us for years. Nic couldn't track movies, so one of us would always be walking around with him, trying to distract him to keep him quiet enough for the rest of us to watch. Now he can track them, but his tastes are so juvenile that it's an act of love to watch with him. I've watched more Disney shows, cartoons, and robot movies than I can stand. Nic says, "Keep me company, Momma," and I'm glued because I'm so thankful that keeping company has become something he cares for.

One of the hardest things for me to let go of was my desire to attend church as a family. Nic simply cannot tolerate the crowd and noise. It has taken me years to address this, and we now are working on ways to introduce him to our church tradition in small, safe amounts.

We were lucky. We were able to get to the bottom of our grief and go on to the next part. The next part was where we truly accepted Nic for who he is and started to plan a new life with normal things like joy and growth in it. They were just served up differently than we expected.

Each of the components of grief—denial, anxiety, depression, anger, and guilt—has its own uniquely destructive face. At times during my growth through all this, I would look up and say to myself, "Oh, this is what denial is" or "This is the slippery than in the books" or " I understand theoretical anger, and I'd like to go back to that now, please, because living it is much too hard."

Denial

Shock danced with denial. We didn't get hit over the head with the diagnosis of autism. It eluded us and the experts for years, although in retrospect I think it was standing in the shadows all the time. At one point we were told specifically that Nic was not autistic. I still look for God's plan in that. Sometimes I think we expected more from Nic than we would have otherwise, and that has supported his growth. But I know some situations would have been easier if I had known what I was dealing with.

I think people tend to go back and forth with the reality of any devastating diagnosis. *Is there something wrong here?* I would ask myself at every well-baby exam, while Nic got further and further behind. *No, no, I must be overreacting. Just be patient.* Meanwhile, my insides were screaming that something was profoundly wrong.

Some of the experts with our case reassured us that there was no significant problem. "Just a language delay and some hyperactivity. Now, if he doesn't start making developmental gains when his speech improves, then we'll have something to worry about." Some just didn't have any opinion, and that was worse, in a way.

Parents react differently. Some hear the truth and can't stand it. Some go diagnosis shopping. By and large, I've found that on the parent acceptability market, ADHD is okay, but Pervasive Developmental Disorders are not. The worst denial from a parent I ever saw in my medical practice resulted in the child being denied any outside help. She homeschooled the child. "He just has severe

ADD. I didn't want him in school with the other kids because they're so mean." *Or maybe you just didn't want him in a system where a more accurate picture of his disabilities would be painted because it's too painful.* I remember the first time anyone got near the word *autism.* I screamed at them. I remember thinking, *I will use my will to make that not so.*

Unfortunately, denial is not only a problem for the families of a child with autism. With invisible disabilities like Autism Spectrum, the medical establishment is often unintentionally in collusion with denial. It's hard to understand how someone who looks so normal and is physically growing normally—with a properly functioning heart, kidneys, liver, and blood—can be so profoundly impaired. The natural preference is to not see it. This is true with lots of other chronic problems, the most insidious of which may be alcoholism.

Anxiety

Anxiety is inherent in modern life. I used to tolerate a high level of it. I make different choices now. Between work, parenting, and wanting time with my husband, the schedule was always full. The disruption and unpredictability of Nic's behavior worsened this. Some mini-crisis would flare up in the office, and I'd get home a half hour late, already tired. The window of opportunity for fixing a meal was lost, and we would try to grab a meal at a restaurant. Nic would balk at the change in routine and, spurred on by hunger, would degenerate into a tantrum. The big kids, mortified, would put their faces in their plates, and Rafael or I would drag Nic screaming out of the restaurant to go hit the closest drive-through with fried chicken nuggets. We eventually learned not to set ourselves up for this, but it required catching on and lots of planning.

I occasionally felt the anxiety friends expressed over seemingly trivial events to be unjustified. I would further isolate myself by thinking, *What would they do if they really had something to worry about?* Complicated by fatigue, this attitude added up to not being able to be a very good friend, which worsened my isolation. All of this looped back and amplified my anxiety. I desperately needed my friends who were not as burdened as I was but who loved me and were capable of empathy. Do you remember the commercial that had a woman saying, "Don't hate me because I'm beautiful"? I needed to learn not to resent my friends with normal or even easy lives. It wasn't their fault that things were easier for them.

I have found that being able to just sit with a friend and listen nonjudgmentally to her concerns is what real friendship is all about. It shouldn't be like "Queen for a Day," the old TV game show where the contestants took turns telling their stories, each more pitiful than the one before. Then the audience would vote with the clap-o-meter. The response would determine who won the Kenmore washing machine and the one-hundred-dollar gift certificate from the Spiegel catalog. I have needed my friends desperately, and they have nurtured me. Often they've been the only balm to my tired, anxious soul. I've found it healing when I can escape myself and listen like that, and when I can be heard like that.

A caution about wolves disguised in friends' clothing: Often the relief of finding someone with similar issues is so great that one's normal discernment process does not operate. There are some very angry, needy people in our crowd. They cannot be real friends if their state is so negative that it sucks energy out of you. Watch out for those who fuel the flame of righteous anger. While that righteous anger may feel energizing momentarily, it usually turns toxic.

I suggest laughter as the discernment test for most friendships. I've found the friendships in which I am able to laugh until I cry to be the richest blessing. I have looked for halos and disguised angel wings. They actually are all around once I've trained my eyes and heart to see them.

As I mentioned before, one of the definitions of anxiety is a hypervigilant state. This is also part of the job description for parents of toddlers and for those responsible for dependent humans of other ages. I found that my anxiety about Nic's physical state was the least grating of the anxieties. I tortured myself endlessly with worries about his future. He is so simple he is profoundly vulnerable. I worried about kids being mean to him. At my most paranoid, I worried about his being sexually exploited. That is a bottomless pit. I fretted endlessly about the day-to-day: *How would I survive at work the next day with so much sleep deprivation? What would I miss, thus harming my patients? What would Nic break next? When would I lose my next babysitter? What if Rafael died and left me all alone?* Or I worried about the big kids' futures: *How extensive would their therapists' bills be? How would this affect their parenting choices? Would I ever have grandchildren?*

Spending that much time in the future, worrying about things over which I had no control, made me sick. I had to get to an end of the energy available for this. I had to learn to put the anxiety aside or it ruined all my interactions. But I had to recognize it for what it was before I could help myself. And this became the pivotal spiritual issue. Who was I going to trust on this one? I experienced a "put up or shut up" spiritual showdown: *For an alleged Christian, where was my faith?* My heart grew and I became capable of a new kind of trust. The single most powerful thing for me still, to cope with anxiety, is prayer. I hasten to add that I pray for other, less self-serving reasons, but there is nothing like spending time in a quiet place with God to adjust my anxiety thermostat. Physical exercise had been enormously helpful also. Now I think of it as a different form of prayer.

Depression

Depression crept in. Sleep deprivation, chronic anxiety, and circumstances over which I had no control were a surefire formula for pulling the endorphin rug out from under me. I lost my insight. I began to believe that things were hopeless. At the worst of it, I lost my voice (hard to believe, I know), which is to say I couldn't ask for help or label what I was experiencing. I became automated. I was a producer. I produced meals and clean laundry and rides to soccer and patient care, but life held no sweetness. Even if I had a moment's rest, I didn't know what to do with it because all my creativity had dried up.

Occasionally I would get a glimpse of something beautiful. Often it would be something in nature like flowers or a sunset. God's easy grace. It would touch me so deeply that a well of feeling would open up, but it would feel like such intense sadness mixed with love that I would be overwhelmed. Feeling nothing often felt better.

Somewhere along the line, I realized that if I didn't learn to take care of myself, I would be unable to care for my children. Or worse yet, I would continue to care for them, and all they would ever see was this crazed, unhappy, angry shrew. It didn't strike me as a recipe for success.

Early psychiatric literature discussed the type of maternal personality that produces an autistic child. This was back when mothers used to make their children schizophrenic too. I think it's human instinct to want to blame someone when things aren't right, and the pseudoscience of early male-dominated psychiatry is no exception. They described cold women with no emotion who responded poorly to their children's needs and were unable to comfort or nurture them. They called them Refrigerator Mothers—and they had the cart before the horse. They were describing clinically depressed women. It would put most of us over the edge if we were locked in a suburban house with a wild, nonverbal, head-banging child who acted deaf and screamed all the time, and no one offered help but we were blamed instead.

I found implementing a program of self-nurture, a gentle therapist, and medications helped move me off of this very stuck-feeling spot.

Many people balk at the suggestion of antidepressant medications. You may think my professional familiarity with these medications may have made me cavalier, but I don't think so. I think it is common for parents not to recognize the true danger their families are in if they become dysfunctional. It's part of the denial. Also, because depression is chronic, parents may not see the big picture easily. Most people who slide into depression get used to feeling crappy, slowly. If they went from their normal selves to their depressed selves in a matter of days, the change would be so glaring and intolerable that it would be perceived as an emergency. You know the popular story about the frog that doesn't jump out of the hot water when it gets turned up a degree at a time.

My personality changes began to affect the other kids, and my marriage deteriorated frighteningly. It was too overwhelming, and I began to feel my family dissolving. This was not in Nic's best interest. I put that data next to taking some relatively safe medications, and in the end it was a no-brainer.

I think if your doctor is trustworthy and suggests antidepressants, run—don't walk—to your closest pharmacy. That is often the change that will enable you to make the other necessary changes, like exercising, praying, and developing your inner resources with the company of kind and stimulating people.

Anger

Anger is complicated. Gender issues confuse the picture. Anger for women is pretty taboo. Depression for men is pretty taboo. I've seen many men who acted chronically angry who were really depressed. I think they learned the anger response as a survival tool when they ran the gauntlet of male adolescence.

Anger is often irrational, like road rage. I've seen this kind of explosion at doctors' offices, public offices like the secretary of state, restaurants (alcohol is gasoline on the fire), and anyplace where these folks feel threatened and have their patience tested. I find it terrifying. In women this is often how PMS anger looks. But there is also rational anger. Injustice produces it.

The systematic, politically-motivated weakening of the public school systems in my state will become life-threatening for the developmentally disabled. This makes me angry. People who take their blessings for granted make me angry. I am angry that I have developed such a judgmental edge inside myself. The question I ask myself is, *How do I transform my anger into constructive action?* It's taken me a while to learn this.

One time, I had just finished working out at the gym. I was hungry and rushing to meet a friend for a sandwich. There were two young women getting dressed next to me. I knew one of them slightly. Ann was a beautiful woman happily parenting a long-awaited two-year-old. We lived in the same neighborhood. She had always seemed a little wild, and I liked her for that. The woman she was talking to must have been in her thirties. She was talking in an authoritative way, telling Ann she needed to get her child's name on the waiting list for all the nursery schools. She was trying to induce competitive panic in my neighbor by implying, *If you don't rush out now and elbow someone else out of the way, you won't get into one of these exclusive clubs and your daughter's life will simply be ruined.*

Then she suggested, "Of course, you could homeschool her." I was thinking, *What's to homeschool a two-year-old? I thought that was what's called living with Mom and Dad.* My sweet neighbor nodded her head and looked a bit dazed at this opinionated woman.

I looked at Ann and said, "Or you can just send her to Glencairn when she's five. It's a perfectly fine school. We have really good public schools."

The other woman chimed in, "Actually, recent studies show that homeschooling is better for children in every respect." Uncharitable thoughts erupted within me. For instance, validation of research methodology and statistical significance didn't look like her cup of tea. The home shopping channel and infomercials about grooming products looked more like her forte.

My face started to flush, and the rest of the visceral anger response spread over my body. I hate feeling that angry. My hungry stomach growled, reminding me that I was in no position to rationally or productively discuss the pros and cons of public education with this woman.

My anger was fed by what I projected about her. Here she was, in the middle of the day, finishing her exercise and grooming hour, with her own child admittedly at some exclusive "waiting list" preschool. She had a big diamond on her hand, and deep inside I was jealous at the amount of leisure she appeared to have.

She typified a movement of the young and rich in my area that has horrified me. These products of the public school system themselves, with their college educations, have created a subculture where they withdraw their considerable resources from the public pool and concentrate on their own narrow interests. Also, the assumption that anyone who puts his mind to it can be a teacher offends me and denigrates a whole profession.

Other assumptions with this package are about all those kids they don't want their kids exposed to. My kid is one of them. That's the real source of the emotional heat that soars through my arteries at such moments. We are dependent on the schools. My child's well-being is tied to the health of the public school system. But my child is no concern of theirs.

One political camp's answer to this kind of problem is often to buy the services you need. Well, I'll tell you, there are a lot of people out there just jumping in line to take care of the elderly and dependent in our society. The wages are so good and the work environment so invigorating. Yeah, right! Being poor or in need is a moral problem in this agenda.

All this flashed through my brain in the time it took me to inhale. But I couldn't go into it with this sheltered, spoiled, self-centered woman because I was about to drop my blood pressure from hunger, and there was every possibility I was not actually perfusing my brain with oxygen.

I turned to the woman and said, "It's not in society's best interest." I looked at Ann and said softly, "Let's talk about this later."

I got out of the changing room without physically assaulting the young woman. It took hours for my temper to settle down. I don't get thrown into those visceral rages often anymore, thank God. I just don't have the nerves for it, and it doesn't help anything. Every once in a while, one sneaks up on me like that. I usually need to eat something.

Guilt

Guilt is a sticky emotion. It gets all over things, is hard to get rid of, and doesn't do a lot of good. It's sort of a cheap, easy response to conflict too. I've never had a conversation with men about guilt and have no intuitive sense of how they process it. My stereotype is that men are able to dump it overboard a bit more effectively than women can. I have a strong sense of the pervasiveness of guilt in many women's psyches. I used to take way too much responsibility for things over which I had no control. It's a package that came with mothering. For the first time, the stakes were so real and the responsibility so vast. I felt guilty before Nic was born about little things, but I elevated it to an art form after he was born. I'm sure the sleep deprivation made this worse, and guilt is a major feature of significant depression.

Mostly I felt guilty about what I'd done to the big kids' lives. I felt bad about the embarrassment they suffered in public with Nic's outbursts. I felt guilty about all the relaxing summer vacations they never had, the spontaneous trips to the ice cream store we never made, the uninterrupted snuggling bedtimes that never were, and the energetic, enthusiastic mother they never knew.

I still feel guilty about Rico. As he will remind me, he can never remember a time when his loud, chaotic brother wasn't there stealing all the attention. Honora, a classic oldest, had four years of being an only child and is pretty adept at getting her needs met. Rico, a classic middle, has waited patiently, observed a lot, and had his kindness and generosity taken for granted more times than we could count. And he is now old enough to play me like a fiddle on this topic.

But this generous habit of feeling like a heel for all the things that have gone wrong in other people's lives can outlast any function it might have had. I took unrealistic responsibility for my kids. I infiltrated their private lives inappropriately and sabotaged their independence. I didn't let go when I should have, because holding on never felt as damaging as the times I wasn't there for them when they needed me. I found guilt to be a first-response emotion, as if it would deflect anger from my loved ones or the judgment of society. *Oh, gee. If I feel bad about this, I will have atoned for my sin,* I would think to myself. Pretty soon I felt bad about everything to sort of keep myself covered. This was not good.

It was, in fact, lazy. (Oh, great—one more thing to feel guilty about!) But retraining my inner self-talk took a huge effort. I had to learn to be gentle and accepting of my personal frailty. Forgiveness is supposed to be a dominant value of my religion. I had trouble practicing it on myself. For parents trapped in grief it may seem like an insurmountable task, but that's because everything feels impossible. The real gut motivator for me was this: If I was treating myself this way, I was teaching my children this pattern also. I found intolerable the image of Honora or Rico talking to themselves with this abusive internal dialogue.

The guilt has a primal quality to it also. It's not that upper-brain-function guilt of religion and society. There is some deep neural programming that reverts to guilt when a person is profoundly depleted. This is seen in severe psychiatric illness and often is a horrible part of dementia. I remember listening to the anxious ramblings of patients with Alzheimer's dementia. These gentle elderly souls trapped in demented bodies worried obsessively about their perceived failings in life. To the outside observer, they had lived full, loving, productive lives. It didn't feel like that to them. Sometimes the guilt with parenting Nic felt like that.

If the guilt doesn't lessen with good self-care, you may need therapy or prayer or both.

Acceptance

Letting a child be a tragedy is a form of disrespect. I think we have to acknowledge the depth of the pain, feel the shock, and process the grief. But then we have to let it go. To wrap a child's whole emotional world in tragedy is a sin. We're not talking hell-and-damnation sin. We're talking sin as a step away from God. To make an innocent child the bearer of the family's entire fate is simply unfair. It's like moms who cling too much and smother their offspring in too much attention. Appropriate separation is healthy and hard to achieve. My dependent, vulnerable Nic seems so needy. But that's the catch. To continue to cast him in this light is a self-fulfilling act.

To let him take risks is one of the hardest things I will ever be asked to do. It would be easier to take the pain myself than see him hurt. But he can't grow without taking those risks. If I don't let him grow to his potential, I really haven't done right by him. My spiritual director says there are two basic issues of faith: There are some for whom belief is the issue and others for whom trust is the issue. This puts my trust to the test.

Rafael and I used to alternate being devastated. I believe taking turns was some mysterious inner-preservation mechanism. The few times we gave over to hopelessness simultaneously, we got way too close to giving up. So we took turns. I would cry and be out of patience and know that things were never going to be better. He would be calm and remind me of whatever progress we had made. Sometimes he had to be creative. Sometimes he really had to scrape around to find something to be optimistic about. Occasionally the attempts would be so pitiful that we would dissolve into desperate laughter.

Then a week later we would trade places. He would sit in the bed, morose, sure that this vulnerable one would never be toilet trained. We would die covered in Nic's feces. Old and gray, someone would open the door to the house and find us petrified in feces, with Nic wandering the house, unbathed, unfed, and crazy. We could sure paint some pictures for ourselves. Then I would point out how Nic hadn't been up in two nights, and didn't that feel good? This was, of course, a real stretch because it takes weeks of an improved sleep habit to actually change the underlying sleep physiology. But we would take anything we could get. It was almost abusive.

Those are the kinds of mind games you play when you're out there. One evening when we were talking in bed, Rafael turned to me and said, "We can do this with grace." He just put that image out there, and it gave us something to shoot for. It was a positive image. In my mind's eye, the sun shone on this image. This was what God wanted for us.

chapter
4 | *Discipline*

*I*n a depleted moment, when I think about these events I cry. In a strong moment, I think about how well I did. Nowhere in my life have I allowed intuition to serve me as I have with mothering. I knew there was something up with Nic from the get-go. This awareness was like a subterranean lava flow. It would bubble up frighteningly and then subside enough to let me get on with my day-to-day life. When it took over, it was almost paralyzing. It was a combination of anger, fear, and dread. We had plenty of problems, and no one seemed to be able to identify them clearly or put the pieces together in a meaningful way. We saw tons of specialists, and they threw in their two cents for their area of expertise only. The whole picture was beyond any of the generalists we saw.

I've often felt that if Rafael and I hadn't both been doctors, we might have gotten help sooner. People project all kinds of stuff onto you when you are associated with these powerful roles. Because we were so uptight, we made them uptight. We tried to be patient. It was difficult to communicate our desperation and the profound nature of how "off" Nic was. The burden of responsibility was depleting. Combined with chronic sleep deprivation, it was life-altering.

Nic was colicky, to say the least. We were unable to find things or routines that helped him. He threw up all the time. Swaddling didn't help. Sometimes motion helped temporarily. Sometimes we repeated things that had helped the day before, and they would make his irritability worse. He was inconsistent and unpredictable. It was maddening. Occasionally people made suggestions, trying to be helpful. This would increase our isolation because all it ever did was reinforce how little those around us understood the complexity of his behaviors and the refractory nature of these problems.

Our family doctor would do his brief developmental assessment, and month after month, year after year, there were huge gaps in Nic's growth. I would ask those same assessment questions to my pediatric patients' parents and would inwardly cringe with their robust answers. Their routine concerns felt so trivial to me. However, a big part of pediatric medicine is to patiently discuss any concerns that are important to new parents. I began to dread seeing children in my practice because of the anger and resentment it stirred up in me. I got nutty about this.

I would sit in Nic's well-baby exams, and my insides would scream, *Do something!* My outside struggled to be calm and patient. Here is the picture: The child is a small toddler, really cute, really hyperactive. He prefers to sit on his mother's shoulders and climb around her neck.

"And what concerns do you have?" the doctor asks. A desperate voice in my head says, *I get no sleep. I experience constant vigilance for this climbing irrational motor unit known as my toddler. I can't turn my head for a second without some destructive or dangerous thing happening. He doesn't comprehend the concept of "no." I am at my wit's end, and I may jump off a bridge if one comes my way today.* What I say is, "Uh, I'm having a lot of trouble getting him to sleep."

"Have you let him just cry?" *Yes, for hours on end.* There is no bottom to the pit of crying and distress this child knows. "Now, Mary, discipline may be hard to instill when you have two other children, but you really must not be a wimp. Get some sort of structured discipline in place."

He may not have actually used the word *wimp.* Part of medical training is getting you in touch with your macho side. I have spent years recovering from the doctor's words, and this emotional memory may be a bit of projection on my part. However, my dad backed up this advice with the classic statement, "Nothing the matter with that boy that a paddle on the behind wouldn't fix."

We got some comfort from the child psychologist when we started working with him. I think Nic was three years old. The psychologist repeatedly assured us that the delays and behaviors were not results of poor parenting. It soothed me to hear this. It started to help me drain away the huge pool of guilt I was drowning in. The guilt was unremitting and polluted multiple interactions. The guilt fueled the anger. The anger also complicated many interactions, like with the school system and medical professionals—the arenas from which I was trying to get help.

I am always surprised when special education people and medical people aren't able to anticipate these emotions. Really exceptional professionals "get" this and have developed techniques for processing and deflecting the guilt and anger. Then it loses much of its mysterious powers.

The child psychologist helped me dump my guilt. He was clear that it was completely irrational on my part. All the energy I was spending feeling guilty would be put to better use doing something positive for this child. He insisted that we had to start getting some sleep or we would never make it. He made some very helpful suggestions.

With autism, it's like there are holes in brain function. The circuitry is simply not there. These kids are incapable of many of the behaviors we expect from them. Because they look normal, many people react to their peculiarities in a judgmental or punitive fashion. This is like yelling at a deaf person or accusing a stroke victim of being willful when he can't walk. Determining the extent of disability is incredibly frustrating because it is so hard to identify the gaps in brain function. There's no simple test or study that can be done. There is no way to get a readout that tells you the exact nature of the child's disability. They can't participate in traditional psychological instruments because those tests use language most of these kids don't have.

Traditional discipline techniques often just don't work. Ironically, the spirit inside autistic individuals is often screaming for structure and consistency. But their traditional communication abilities are so blunted that they resort to bizarre behaviors in an attempt to be heard.

Wanda, an autism consultant for our schools, told me a story. She was called in to make suggestions for handling some aggressive behavior in a student. He was biting. She designed an old-fashioned behavior modification program, and soon the child stopped biting. He started kicking. They worked with him to stop kicking, and he started scratching and pinching. The problem with behavior modification was that it did nothing to help the child process the emotion that he was unable to express verbally. They finally got everyone in the classroom to help him identify when he was angry, and then he would go out into the hall and kick the doormat.

For us, the behavior problems couldn't be addressed until some other things were in place. The simplicity of the things that eventually did make a difference shocked me.

chapter
5 | *Sleep*

I remember talking to a friend of mine in the park at the worst of it. She is a family practice doctor also. She said her review of the literature showed tales of women who likened sleep to gold. It became the most prized object in their lives. The physical effects of long-term sleep deprivation are devastating. In the long run, it produces personality changes.

My body ached from morning till night. I had characteristic fibromyalgia. Having and treating it is a doctor's nightmare because it is so lifestyle-related. How could I lower my stress when the major stressor was my child? In retrospect, I could have hired a babysitter and gone to the gym. My work ethic, however, wouldn't even allow me to consider that. This is an example of an internal preprogrammed opinion that had to change in order for me to survive.

Nic went for years without any pattern. He would occasionally sleep through the night, but our sleep patterns were so shot, we couldn't enjoy that. We were waking up to hear if anything horrible was going on. When he was eighteen months old, I found him in the garage in the middle of the night. It was subzero January. For a gross-motor-delayed individual, that kid sure could climb out of his crib. The step up to the house from the garage put the door handle just out of his reach. He was almost blue he was so cold. I've never figured out what noise woke me up.

Eventually, at the suggestion of the psychologist, we installed a plain old hook-and-loop lock on the outside of his door. The psychologist reassured us that this was the responsible thing to do. We had no other way to safely contain him, and we had to start getting some sleep. Having the psychologist's permission to do this, and trusting him, was a major step for Rafael and me.

When we moved, all the doors had wonderful old keys that worked. Of course, the problem with that was two other children. We lost keys with children both inside and outside of rooms. The most embarrassing episode involved borrowing an extension ladder from some neighbors two blocks over. They still tease me about it. After losing keys on more than one occasion, the locksmith finally sold me a really good skeleton key.

This was the beginning of some semblance of routine. Usually, after endless efforts to establish a bedtime ritual that would soothe Nic to sleep, we would give up in exhaustion and listen to him cry himself to sleep. This often took hours. But at least we knew where he was and that he was safe.

One of the reasons Nic had so much trouble sleeping was that he had reflux (vomiting up from the stomach) so badly that he choked himself awake every night. We eventually got effective help with that from medication, and he was able to establish a sleep pattern. When he started to sleep, we started to sleep. It took about seven years.

Sometimes he still has middle-of-the-night craziness. This is usually a flag that something isn't right. Sometimes it's because his medications are off or some change in his school or home routine has rocked the boat. Sometimes I'm sure it's the spin of the planet.

When he does wake up, it usually involves quite a display of energy. He comes loudly into our room, maniacally cheerful. He flips the lights on and loudly proclaims what he wants, which usually involves getting one of us out of bed. Like "I'm hungy, Momma!" or "Wanna watch Capin Planet," or he just wants to talk. I have such reflexive fear of sleep deprivation that I go into a militaristic stance immediately. I liken myself to a POW who was brainwashed in Korea during the 1950s. The mere hint of getting close to this trauma invokes all kinds of phobic behavior.

I am now a very aggressive, you might even say militant, sleeper. I protect my nine o'clock bedtime like gold. I flaunt this behavior. I rub my hands together in glee when I know there are no evening commitments and I might even make it to bed by eight-thirty. I don't go to sleep at this time but revel in my inaccessibility. The children may come and make supplication at the bed of the queen, and I may or may not grant them an audience.

Actually, I always grant them an audience. In bed is the place where I am most relaxed. Most of my good conversations with the kids occur while I'm there. They know they have to get in with me, and I may even demand snuggling. This practice evolved because of the trauma of prolonged sleeplessness.

When I reflexively respond to Nic's nocturnal demands in a scrappy, pick-a-fight fashion, he usually counters by digging in his heels. If Rafael deals with it, everything is calmer. I don't freak out, and Nic is allowed to save face. For a kid with a disability that's supposed to blunt his social awareness, he sure has some complicated behaviors. We have found that with all disputes, we must find a solution that allows him to save face. This is good training for conflict resolution with anyone.

We have on occasion had the good fortune to get him to turn off the light when he wakes up in the middle of the night. We advise him of the location of the desired video, book, or stuffed animal. He goes away and entertains himself until he falls asleep again. With luck we are back to sleep in five minutes. Truthfully, I am back to sleep in five. Rafael's sleep will have been completely disrupted, so he watches CNN or reads or goes to the gym early. I don't know if it's discipline on his part or temperament, but he seems to be able to make it through the day without falling apart the way I do. This is one reason why it takes at least two adults to raise kids. With someone like Nic, it takes at least two adults, multiple sibs, cousins, uncles, aunties, friends, teachers, and angels.

With the return of sleep, we were actually able to start making decisions again. The chronic anxiety lessened. This was one of those little things that added up to a huge improvement in our quality of life. I believe it was only then that we started being able to move forward instead of cycling around with the same intractable problems and nonsolutions. We were able to move on to new difficulties.

| *Tantrums*

*T*he tantrums are these awful neurologic explosions that go off unexpectedly. Sometimes, in retrospect, we can see that we should have predicted them. We used to kick ourselves or bang our heads against the wall for being so stupid as not to have seen them coming. I am gentler with myself now for not having complete precognition about these events. It has made life simpler for the whole family since Rafael and I stopped taking responsibility for things over which we have no control, like world affairs, plane schedules, and delays at train tracks. However, the tantrums are horrible, and it is very human to wish to control any factor that contributes to them.

I believe the tantrum behavior is interwoven with the brain areas that contribute to obsessions and compulsive behaviors. Somehow they are related. Wanda the autism specialist says the tantrums are most often triggered by sensory overload. When we have gone back and reconstructed the circumstances leading up to them, this is often true. But sometimes they seem to come out of the blue, and we are left with our jaws slack, wondering what hit us.

The tantrums are the events that have traumatized the family the most. The fear of them sculpts our life. New places, smells, noises, and routines can all precipitate them. Routine events—like going to the grocery store, a movie, or out to dinner—can become a tightrope walk. Often much-needed relaxation activities provoke tantrums. Like vacation. So it's a form of catch-22. You need to relax to cope. The things you do to relax provoke depleting behavior. This can become mental torture.

If we don't plan ahead and have food available at appropriate times in acceptable places, the whole stack of cards can come crumbling down. If the rhythm of the day doesn't go just right with the appropriate expenditure of exercise calories and consumption of cartoon calories, we pay with sweat and frustration.

The irony in this is that no one loves a vacation more than Nic does. He seems to need a break in routine as much as he thrives on routine. It's kind of like this back-and-forth cycle between stable routine, during which he consolidates his skills, and adventures, through which he gathers new data and experience. After a successful trip we often see a burst of maturation. This growth pattern is similar for the big kids, but they don't have tantrums when things go wrong by half a degree. Many of the most memorable tantrums are related to coming home from trips. Our psychologist says "duh" to this: "Who likes to come back from vacation?"

The trip to Spain went more smoothly than any of us had anticipated. I had wanted to take the kids to the Alhambra ever since our honeymoon there. I thought the Moorish-flavored castle with all its legends would fascinate young boys. Even on our honeymoon, some part of me knew we would have boys. That part of the trip went fine. The few days on the Costa del Sol were actually pretty refreshing. The orange trees in the plaza were in fragrant bloom. The chocolate and churros were a hit with the whole family. Nic even waited in some lines without losing his self-control or becoming agitated. It was a miracle for us all. We flew back to New York City, excited that we might have other adventures like this in the future. We spent the night with my sister and brother-in-law. The next morning we walked to the Central Park Zoo. We figured we were home free.

The zoo was small and had no alligators. This was very disappointing to Nic. This was, in fact, huge for Nic. He got more and more desperate to find the alligators. We could see the self-control drain out of him. We figured he might be hungry, so we abandoned the image of the fabulous little lunch my sister had in mind and went over to the armory lunchroom. There were sandwiches, soup, pop, and chips. We thought it would do. Not for Nic. He started speaking louder and louder. Then he started screaming and sobbing. The place was not crowded, but the staff looked on in disgust, shock, and discomfort. Rafael and I became more and more agitated. When Nic senses that, it's like throwing gasoline on the fire. I always think about how they say horses can sense when they have an inexperienced rider. I'd like to know what kind of wave transmits this data to horses and to kids like Nic.

My sister, her husband, and the other kids experienced what I call "secondary mortification." That is when you are involved because the people you are with are having this horrible scene, but you are powerless to do anything about it. In fact, any attempts at intervening make it worse. My big kids have had to endure more of this than I can stand to acknowledge. While it has been painful, they have learned a lifetime of compassion and sensitivity.

Enter the Evil One. If she had been to the costume department before this scene, she couldn't have dressed more perfectly for her part. She was petite, with gray hair swooped up in a tight, orderly beehive. Her gray suit was perfectly tailored. It said "restrained power." Her face was made up perfectly with foundation, lipstick, and mascara. It functioned as a perfect armor, keeping her guarded from humanity. Her bifocals were hip. She communicated control and perfection with all of her being. She walked angrily down the hall. She looked at us over her glasses, inspecting us. Apparently we inadequately comprehended the moral implications of allowing a child to scream in public like this. She was outraged. How could we allow this? She said, "You must quiet him down. People are trying to work!"

Rafael and I had to physically carry Nic out. We used what we call "the bum's shuffle": one adult on each side, with one hand around the upper arm just under the armpits and the other under the elbow. Then you lift the body up, just high enough so the feet can't touch the ground. The feet can run in midair or kick, but they are effectively taken out of commission for locomotion.

When things get that bad, Nic loses all self-control and becomes a kicking, screaming, biting two-year-old. But he's not two. He's bigger. Nine-year-old bites and kicks hurt. When this happens, I often flash to the future and wonder what it's going to be like when he's thirty. After an event like this, we all are wiped out. We went back to the apartment, picked up our luggage, and got into the car my sister had called for. I gave the driver the wrong airport, and we took off.

Other memorable tantrums have had various excruciating

characteristics. The degree to which they are public is the hardest detail, but duration and destructiveness are parameters as well.

A little tantrum that cousin Eeva remembers, and she tells this story as though it is a fond memory, occurred the night of my parents' sixtieth wedding anniversary. All the grown-ups were out to dinner, and Eeva was staying with the boys to have pizza under the responsible eye of a kind, but green, babysitter. The landscape project, which Nic loved, had been going on for weeks. Kirby the landscaper even left the little baby bulldozer in the yard. Nic liked to sit in it and pretend. Unfortunately, someone left the keys in it that evening. Nic got in under Heather the babysitter's supervision. She was okay until he turned the thing on. She tried to get him out of the vehicle, but he wouldn't budge. Sensing a precarious situation, he went over the edge. She started crying. The sainted neighbor Jeff came over and manually extracted the screaming Nic. Sometime in all this, the pizza arrived. Eeva's favorite detail in all this was how Winnie the hound got right up on the table and ate the pizza *and* Nic's medicine, which had been left out on the table. After a frantic call, we got home to find another sainted neighbor, who is actually a teacher at Nic's school, soothing them all.

The longest tantrum occurred on the way back from Chicago during one of the most sublime vacations we've ever had. Nic was awesome for most of the trip. We stayed in a hotel on Wacker Drive with a great view of the river. He loved the outdoor art on Michigan Avenue. He even tolerated some public dining.

We took one of the riverboat trips at night under the stars. The August air was hot and humid with a fresh breeze off the lake. The buildings were huge urban dinosaurs decked with jewels. Our whole family was together, happy doing the same thing, woven into a magical moment. Those have been rare events. We should have known something was coming.

The next day we all got lucky at the discount mall on our way to St. Joe's. We gloated over our shoes, underwear, shirts, and pocketknife. We were going to stay in a small hotel that over-looked the lake. They gave us a suite that, we found out later, did not have the promised view of the lake. I had specifically asked for a view of the lake, so I requested they switch our rooms. By this time the kids had looked around, and Nic had decided where he was going to sleep. The news that we would have a view of the lake in the new rooms meant nothing to him. He started to go into orbit. He just didn't want to change rooms. That tantrum lasted almost twenty-four hours, with about four hours off for sleep. The volume was controllable for some reason, and we didn't get kicked out of the hotel. We couldn't go to a restaurant with Nic screaming, so we got junk food from a party store and feasted on Doritos and pop in the room. No one commented on the lovely view of the lake.

That tantrum prompted Rico to come up with the idea of a poison, or at least a medicated dart, that we could shoot through a straw to drop Nic in his tracks. I do not believe such a dart really exists, but that was so horrible an episode that it prompted us to experiment with tranquilizers under Nic's physician's supervision. Nothing has worked like magic, and the most effective tranquilizer takes two hours to kick in, but at least we know we have something that can help interrupt the cycle. Before we had that ace up our sleeve, our hackles would be up during every vacation, waiting for the bomb to drop. This, of course, completely undid the intent of our vacations, which was to relax.

I am pleased to report that Nic has had only one tantrum during which he was destructive. He was so mortified that later, in what I call "the hangover stage," he tried to Scotch tape back onto the house the vinyl siding he had hacked off. It was siding less than a year old.

The most public tantrum took place in a movie theater. Nic loves the movies. He pays attention to the previews and anticipates the opening of many movies. He can tell me the opening dates of any kid movie for the next nine months. He waited twelve months for *The Grinch* to come out after seeing it advertised at *Stuart Little*. He talked about it at least once a week for a year.

We had anticipated this particular movie for about six months. It came out in the summer. He knew the day it was to open and had his heart set on seeing it that day. I made a terrible error in judgment and took him to the five o'clock show. He was adequately fed, but all his concentrating medicine had worn off. The place was packed. By the time the previews started, there were no empty seats. We managed to get seats in the very back row, which is his favorite. He likes his back to a wall. When the movie started, he couldn't settle down. He asked me repeatedly about who were the good guys and who were the bad guys, his voice rising. The softer I needed his voice to be, the louder it got. The more stressed I got, the more he repeated himself. The mutterings and side-glances of our neighbors grew increasingly sharp. I knew Nic wasn't going to be able to get it together.

I lured him out of the theater with the promise of popcorn and a candy bar. When we got out into the hall, I explained that we couldn't go back in because he couldn't be quiet enough. He started to sob and scream. Then he started to lie on the floor and kick his feet. Eventually he tried to run back into the theater, and I had to physically restrain him.

This went on for a very long time, with the volume swelling. Fortunately, there weren't a lot of people around. Finally, some security guards came by and asked me what was up. They started with the "you've-got-a-problem-lady" tone, but after observing the scene, they soon switched to the "what-can-we-do-to-help" tone. They could tell that I was on the verge of tears. I asked them to help me get Nic outside. They gave him what I considered to be a very professional bum's shuffle. He was so shocked that I allowed strangers to touch him this way, and they were so big and had on such cool uniforms, that he stopped screaming. I called Rafael and asked him to come pick up Nic in the car. I thought Nic was so crazy that if I tried to drive him by myself, he might do something dangerous like hit me or open the car while it was moving.

There was some walkie-talkie talk between the security guards and the manager about what degree of damage had been done. They were discussing whether they were going to have to give refunds to the rest of the movie audience or something. Rafael arrived just in time. Nic settled down once he was in his papa's car. I got in my car and cried and drove around until sunset. These events hung in the air for days afterward.

The tantrum I handled the best was recent. This must mean I am trainable. We were in a sporting goods store, looking to replace the backpack Nic had had for several years. When he gets attached to an object—like his favorite shoes, pajamas, backpack, mushroom pillow (a hand-sewn pillow with fabric containing pictures of mushrooms), or blanket—he will use it until it is literally falling apart.

He thought that if we went to the same store we could simply replace the Godzilla backpack, which had been purchased just after the movie came out. The idea of this being dated material meant nothing to him. He started to raise his voice while we were in the store. The customers and staff stared at us. I didn't flap. I asked him to come outside with me and we would see if there was one at the store next door. He fell for it. When we got outside, I explained to him that it was not okay to have a tantrum and that shouting and crying in a store are not appropriate behaviors. I acknowledged that he was angry and sad to lose his long-term backpack, but we were not going to find one just like it because they didn't make Godzilla stuff anymore. He actually seemed to listen to some of this, but it didn't turn the tide.

We were standing on a covered section of sidewalk between the two stores. He started to accelerate the stomping and screaming. I told him that wasn't okay, turned my back, and walked to the car. That stopped him for a moment. I've never actually left him like that. The car was only about four parking spaces away, so this wasn't real abandonment on my part, but it was physically farther apart than we usually are when he is flipping out. He was quiet.

I got in the car and moved it to the fire lane right in front of his piece of sidewalk. I listened to music and intermittently lowered the window to ask if there was anything I could do to help him. He alternated between just standing there, lying on the sidewalk kicking his heels, screaming, and crying pitifully. Customers walked by with a variety of glances, most of them uncomfortable at seeing such a distressed kid. In the car, I didn't have to receive their disapproving glares about my obviously pathologic and inept parenting, and I was warm. Nic was not. Every time I lowered the window to inquire about his state of mind, he would burst into a tirade or cry crocodile tears. Both of these behaviors would stop when I put the window up. It was fascinating. After about forty minutes, he walked over to the van and got in. He was tired, cold, and hungry. We got him some McDonald's, and he finished off the rest of the tantrum at home at about half-steam. We still haven't purchased a new backpack. It's a touchy subject for both of us.

He often impresses me with his self-control during his frustrating day-to-day existence. He tries and tries to get people to understand him. He struggles immensely with reading and writing. He shows remarkable persistence. In some ways I'm surprised he doesn't have more tantrums than he does. I think I would.

When he is caught in the throes of one of these episodes, it really is like he is possessed, and I am thankful the behaviors haven't been more destructive. Only when he is physically approached, as in the bum's shuffle, will he attack another person. He bit Rafael and me when we had to carry him out of the armory in New York. Fortunately, he didn't bite the movie security guards. He knew I asked them to help me. I would like to think he would defend himself if he were ever assaulted. Wanda says that is an appropriate fight-or-flight response.

It's best to leave him alone when he's having a tantrum so he won't hurt other people. He does harm himself on occasion. I have seen him bite himself in rage. I have seen him so frustrated that he bangs his head or pinches himself. The occupational therapist thinks the head banging is some sort of deep stimulation to the central nervous system and it paradoxically may soothe him. It is horrible to see your child harm himself.

It makes me feel empathy for the parents of teenagers who mutilate themselves when struggling with depression, anger, or other craziness. Sometimes I think that it might be worse for them. For people with a pretty normally functioning kid, this kind of behavior could be quite shocking.

chapter
7 | *Obsessions and Compulsions*

Where's Waldo?

We like to go out walking on the weekends. It runs off some of the "piss and vinegar." Nic can go for hours, and if the weather is right, so can I. One Saturday afternoon, Michigan State, our home team, was playing Illinois. A huge Big Ten football game is like a carnival. Nic usually doesn't like the crowds or the noise. Neither do I.

We went to his favorite McDonald's, which has two stories. We had the usual meal. Upstairs we can look out at all the cars and the sunlight and the sky.

We walked home a different way than usual. I was trying to steer Nic away from all the activity. We were halfway up M.A.C. Avenue (Michigan Agricultural College, so named before the GI bill boomed us up to a university) when he realized this was the street of his beloved Neely. She had been our babysitter for two years. She is awesome. He wanted to see her. I explained that she was not at home. She was at the football game, along with eighty thousand other people. This didn't mean anything to him. His insistence that we could find her was an example of his obsessive behavior. If he is caught in the web of an obsession, he seems motivated to overcome phobias and display competent behaviors we've not seen before. These obsessions seem to energize him.

He decided he wanted to go to the football game and find Neely. I reminded him that there would be lots of people and noise. He didn't care. When he's caught up in an obsession, he believes he can bend reality to suit himself. He wanted to find Neely.

We turned around and went back to the campus. The crowds were starting to leave their seats. MSU was not winning, so some people were trickling out early. The announcer's voice echoed off the buildings like we were in a canyon. We went to the river. You could feel in the air the increased density of people, even though the crowds had not started leaving in earnest. Then we heard the ending noises, several cheers followed by ahs of disappointment. The crowd started streaming out. We positioned ourselves on the stairs at one end of a bridge that is a major egress. It was like watching a river of people. Soon the bridge was overflowing. We saw church friends, former patients of mine, Nic's swimming teacher, and even old friends from grade school, but no Neely.

The crowd started to thin out. The marching band went by. The bridge was empty. We crossed over to be nearer to the stadium with its residual crowd. Nic was searching all the faces. He had been searching all the faces on the bridge, especially every blond. We walked around the stadium. The crowds had really thinned. There were some die-hard tailgaters, and we were offered chips and popcorn. But Nic couldn't be distracted; he was starting to get it.

I saw his face sadden. His posture got pre-tantrum. He finally said to me in the most pitiful voice, "It like Where Waldo, Mom, but it not fun." It took me a few seconds to fully understand what he was saying. Waldo is the character we search for in the *Where's Waldo?* books. He is this tiny character hidden in pages full of similar tiny characters engaged in some zany activity. Nic always finds him first. He's good at that game. This reality had fallen painfully short of his expectations. He had been unable to "will" Neely's appearance.

A sign of his growth is that he postponed his tantrum until no one was around, and it was fairly discreet and short-lived. Partly, I think, because he had to pee, and lying on the concrete sidewalk and kicking your heels in late October is pretty cold.

We started walking toward home. We walked by a few student bars packed with mourning fans. Nic was still scanning all the crowds, even those in the bars. Suddenly we thought we saw her! We saw from behind a tall thin woman with blunt-cut blond hair. We mashed our faces up to the window. We were not subtle. The woman's head changed angle slightly and I saw the cigarette. It was not Neely. She turned just enough for us to see her full profile, and then Nic knew it was not Neely. He was crestfallen and hung his head as we slogged on home.

He said, "Momma, it like Jessica Rabbit."

"What do you mean?"

"Remember when Eddie Valiant go to Toontown?" he said. I did remember, in exact detail, because we have watched *Roger Rabbit* a million times. Eddie goes into Toontown looking for Roger and Jessica Rabbit. He goes up the animated elevator in a tall building with a hound dog elevator operator. He trips going in and out of the elevator. They use every conceivable elevator sight gag. He walks down the animated hall and opens the animated door where we see the voluptuous animated Jessica Rabbit from behind in her skintight red gown. She turns around slinkily, and instead of the beautiful Jessica, it is someone with an ugly, big-lipped, bucktoothed face. Eddie is, of course, shocked and somehow gets pushed out the animated window and falls several stories, during which he is the brunt of several more sight gags committed by Tweetie Bird, Mickey Mouse, and a few other famous animation stars. Nic knows this sequence by heart. Now we have lived it.

We finally got home, and instead of throwing a really ferocious tantrum, Nic was just sad and tired. So, ultimately, the walk had been a success, and he had once again astounded me with all he had going on in that captive little brain.

Compulsions

Nowadays, you can read good magazine articles about common psychiatric illnesses. Lots of people are relieved when they find out that some of their peculiar habits may actually have a diagnosis. Obsessive Compulsive Disorder (OCD) is one of these diagnoses. I think the obsessions are what go on in the mind, and the compulsions are the behaviors that result from the obsessions. Adults I have worked with who have OCD are often tremendously relieved to have a physiological explanation for these habits. With medicine and appropriate psychotherapies, this disorder often can be treated very effectively.

Lots of my patients tell stories about how these behaviors developed during childhood. Sometimes they were rewarded for their behaviors, like young women who clean too much. Sometimes they just kept the habits "in the closet," like hand-washers. Adults seek help when they can no longer keep the habits invisible, like spending three to four hours a day on their washing routines. Sometimes they read about these problems and have an epiphany that not everyone lives this way. Adults usually have the advantage of some insight and a brain that works fairly well in other areas. Kids with retardation don't have these tools.

We are almost to the point where we can laugh about most of Nic's habits. The degree of compulsive behaviors we have lived with far surpasses any of the behaviors my adult patients described to me.

Touching

When we started Nic on medicine to help these behaviors, he couldn't walk across a room without touching multiple surfaces. He would actually have to walk from side to side in the room—touching the countertops, floor, and walls—before he could get to the other end of the room. Stacey, the occupational therapist, says Nic gets information about the world through touching. The guard at the Chicago Art Institute didn't seem too interested in that explanation when Nic went for some of the Impressionists' paintings. I, myself, thought this showed excellent taste on his part. Unfortunately, we only recently discovered the part of the museum that is designed for touchers. I think their biggest constituency is the blind, but people with really active kids need to know about the place.

The medicines have really helped the physical behaviors that were compulsive. They haven't been too helpful with the obsessions.

Clothes

One of Nic's big obsessions has to do with clothes. I think this may have developed from his tactile hypersensitivity. Nic loves pajamas. I think the tight but stretchy cloth minimizes stimulation to his skin. He also has been obsessed with Batman since he was a preschooler. The obvious ecstatic union of these two obsessions was Batman pajamas. I bought them by the half dozen. There was a stretch of two or three years during which he would wear only Batman pajamas and black cowboy boots.

The cowboy boot thing went on for longer than the pj's. One good side of the cowboy boots was that I could go shoe shopping for him in about five minutes, except that the drive to the cowboy store with the plastic horse and all the cool bridles and tack was about twenty-five minutes into farm country. I preferred to make the drive in the spring or fall because I got to see the open fields, which made me feel briefly serene. When we arrived at the store, Nic knew the drill by heart. We would get out of the car and smell the cow and horse dung rich in the air. Then we would enter the store. On the left were all the expensive horse toys for collectors. One year he actually talked me into buying a plastic Palomino for an exorbitant amount of money.

We would turn to the right and walk through the room with the brightly striped horse blankets, glittering tack, and life-size plastic horse. He always wanted to get on the horse. They would kick us out in two seconds if he did. Then we would walk through the next room, where there must have been three hundred hats. One year, all Honora wanted for her birthday was a cowboy hat. She looked awesome in it. For sentimental reasons I still have Nic's red hat. One of my favorite Christmas pictures is of the whole family dolled up. Nic is in his father's arms in his pj's, black boots, and red cowboy hat.

The next room over was the boot room. My personal best buy there was half-price purple cowboy boots that fit like a glove. Often Nic would start to get antsy. The challenge became fitting the boots as fast as we could. At times when I had a sib with me, we even resorted to tackling Nic down and grabbing his foot as the saleslady held up different sizes to the bottom of his foot. She would do this in rapid succession as we eyeballed the size. Sometimes he would actually try them on, but not usually. I often felt like I had competed in some equivalent of rodeo calf tying, only it was my little human. Sometimes I leaped up victorious to the cheers of the invisible crowd and bowed and acknowledged the incredible skill I had displayed. Other times I wasn't so victorious. It usually depended on the sense of humor of the saleslady.

The incredible selection of boots for toddlers on up distracted me. The smaller and more ornate the boot, the more I tried to figure out how to justify buying them. Red with white cutouts, side fringe, silver on the toes, and tabs spoke volumes to something inside me. Then the cowboy shirts would distract me, and if I had the big kids with me, they would start to cringe, worried I might actually buy one and wear it.

By now, both Nic and I would be overstimulated by all the visuals in the store. I'd be dazed, but he would be off-the-wall. I would struggle to refocus, cash out, and get home. He was often so attached to his cowboy boots that he wouldn't give them up, even when there were holes in the soles and heels. The most dramatic episode was when he wore a hole through the hollow heel and gravel kept slipping in so that he eventually ended up walking on rocks. He still wouldn't give up those boots, even for new ones sitting in the closet.

He has been very resistant to changes in his clothing routines. This is something the big kids have had lots of opinions about because he has often looked so peculiar. If we ever wanted him to try something new, I would put Honora on the job. She has always had a talent for talking him into clothes he would not otherwise wear. He tolerates all kinds of grooming if she is the one administering it. He'll put up with a lot to get attention from her. When he was little, she would dress him up in capes and costumes and put gel in his hair. Now he tries to do this to the poor dog, who puts up with anything to get attention from him.

Construction Equipment

The obsessions associated with autism are frequently described as "having a very narrow range of interests." What an understatement! The very first thing I could do to entertain or distract Nic was to draw pictures of construction equipment. I drew as we waited for doctor appointments. I drew at restaurants. I have drawn at least twenty thousand "digger cranes" in the last twelve years. I'm quite good at it. As Nic's language has developed, we are more accurate in what we call what I'm drawing, but we're still drawing the same old pictures. Now he calls them excavators, and on a really focused day, I draw bulldozers, pickup trucks, semis, cranes, tower cranes, and pile drivers. I have a master's degree in Tonka.

We have been entertained for hours watching heavy equipment. We even have friends who report in when they have spotted an interesting construction site. On our last trip to Chicago, all of Wacker Drive was under construction. Nic likes his hotel rooms up as high as possible. He spent hours lying on the window ledge, looking down at the river and all the equipment at work. I get vertigo describing the scene. He loved it. His aunt did an oil painting of a backhoe one year for his birthday. It hangs in his room above his extensive collection of wheeled objects.

Room Preference

I never knew there were so many forces at play in a room. Nic's sensitivities in this area are like a psychic feng shui. He prefers a small room to a large one. If we are in a busy restaurant, I position him so he is looking at the smallest part of the room. The best thing is if we can be seated in the back and with him facing a back wall. Positioning him in this way wipes out a bunch of overstimulating visual data.

Noise is a big factor in how acceptable a space is. For a while we tried ear protectors like some people use on the line in a factory. They helped him get through some Christmas Eve services at church. He also used these at the beginning of evenings at a bowling alley, and then as he got used to the noise, he could take them off.

He likes doors closed—all of them, if possible. He likes to go back upstairs to check that I haven't secretly opened any doors to let light into the hallway. He can hear if a door is closed completely or not. He will send me back to close the door again if he doesn't hear the latch click. I send him back to do it now. I figure if it's his obsession, he can get out of the chair.

Food

Wanda the autism specialist and Stacy the occupational therapist say that anything fried and crunchy is autism food. I believe this is true. When Nic first started to emerge as a personality with interests, his major focus was McDonald's. It is the first word he ever read. He learned brand logos before he had much speech, which is no surprise because he is predominantly a visual learner. He has now generalized this fondness to all fast food. He knows what the latest toy is at each franchise and has been known to abandon any brand allegiance he occasionally adopts to get the movie character of his latest obsession.

"Chicken Nugget Happy Meal Sprite As the Drink No Sauce No Ketchup" is the only reward we've ever found effective with our attempts at old-fashioned behavioral modification. The whole sentence comes out now on cue at the ordering window. I've given this order a thousand times. They're usually not used to getting this much information in one scoop and invariably ask me if I want ketchup or sauce. Whether it's a reward for him or a convenience for me, that boy loves chicken nuggets.

It's got to be the same, however. Each time it has to be exactly the same. "Chicken Nugget Happy Meal Sprite As the Drink No Sauce No Ketchup" in the white bag. On more than one occasion, receiving it in a brown bag has driven him over the edge. For a while I drove around with a backup white bag just in case we ran into a franchise that was out of them. I have on rare occasion been able to distract him with something long enough to make the switch into the correct bag. Sometimes that doesn't work and we end up with all kinds of sobbing and misery. I have driven late into the night in search of the right bag or the right toy or the right whatever. There were times I would just drive, hoping to tire him out or bore him into getting interested in something else or falling asleep.

Cars

Automobile seating was one of his weirdest obsessions. When Nic was about two years old, we sold the little station wagon and purchased a real minivan. It was huge compared with what we were used to. Nic soon found his favorite place in the way-back trunk area. There is no seat belt there, but of course it became the only place he would sit. And he wouldn't just hop into the back of the car and sit or lie there; he needed his objects all in just the right places. The number of objects he needed before he could ride in peace increased to the point of the ridiculous.

It started with wanting his blanket and pillow. The blanket was a twin-sized comforter, not a baby blanket. The pillow was a complicated arrangement. The first layer was a standard pillow, with a patchwork pillow that had been handmade for me eons ago laid on top of that. One of the prints on the patchwork has mushrooms on it, so it is called the mushroom pillow. Now remember, Nic was a vomiter. The blanket and pillows were washed hundreds of times. Eventually the pillow and comforter lost all their stuffing. As these objects got thinner and easier to transport, he started to add stuffed animals and books to his entourage.

Eventually it would take me about ten minutes to get him packed in the car.

It wasn't like we could just say, "Hey, let's go to the ice cream store," and have the family hop in the car and go get ice cream. We would have to search the house to find where all these things had scattered to, as Nic would play with them in the house in between car rides. While we layered him into the back with his blankie, pillows, Baguira, Simba, and whatever books we were devouring that week, I would have a silent conversation with myself. I would practice explaining to the emergency room doctors we would surely end up seeing why he wasn't seatbelted in. I would also practice having a similar conversation with the police officers who never stopped us. I am thankful for that.

Eventually he let me use packing crates to transport his stuff. When he added the second crate to the program, I started to dream of a new car.

We went out one afternoon when the van was about nine years old and looked at new cars. I was awestruck at the change in technology. We looked at one that had a video player in it. The salesman was practically throwing the car at us. No money down, no interest, no payments for some absurd amount of time. The inside was leather.

We took it for a spin. We drove up to the house, and the kids ran out, gleeful. Rico got in, glanced at the dashboard, and looked me in the eye: "You know, this car has more computer capability in it than the entire Apollo space program." Well, thank you, dear— I had no idea.

Nic got in the car and there was awe on his face. He climbed into the far backseat on the right side. He put on the seat belt without being told and started running his hands over the leather, back and forth, back and forth. It was like he was in a sacred space. Then he saw the video screen. Joy spread over his face.

"Momma, we gettin' this car?"

"If you promise to sit in that seat and wear your seat belt every time you get in this car, we can get it."

"Yes, Momma."

He has been true to his word. He gets in the back and puts on his seat belt without being told. He often reminds us to do the same. He also requests that I lock the doors each time we take off. He needs to hear that click. If for some reason his father delays putting his own belt on, Nic becomes agitated and I can't get out of the driveway without a commotion. He has us well trained by now.

Nail Cuticles

Nail cuticles are something few parents need to spend much time on. In our world they are huge. For some reason, Nic picks his. I have had lots of friends and patients who were nail-biters. This is thought to be one of those "out there," genetically-programmed fixations. Nic leaves his nails alone but picks his cuticles. The thin little strips of skin get torn and often bleed. Then he picks the scabs. It makes me wince to watch this. Wanda the autism expert says she thinks this is a common autism thing. My friend Steve the psychologist thinks that somehow some serotonin neurotransmitter pathway is triggered by this behavior, and so it reinforces itself.

Now we are into Band-Aids big-time. The ritual goes like this: Band-Aids go on in the morning after breakfast. Nic uses his hands a lot at school, and sometimes the Band-Aids fall off or get replaced. He often does a little picking there. At bedtime we take all the Band-Aids off and let the fingers "rest." Often he likes me to rub a little cream on his cuticles. If he lets me do this regularly, there is less tearing. In the morning he has his bath and breakfast, and we start all over again.

When he first started to use the Band-Aids, he resisted letting us change them. They would begin to smell, and we would sneak up on him in his sleep and peel them off. The underlying skin was pale and macerated. I waited in fear of the day he would become ill from a skin infection. I could see myself explaining this one to the doctor in the pediatric intensive care unit as they pumped Nic full of medication to save his life.

Language

Perseveration is a term used for repetitive language. The urge for Nic to do this is uncontrollable. It is like a language compulsion. We say things over and over. Yes, he has me repeating things now too. The wording has to be just right, and I have to hold up my end of the conversation in his carefully constructed word patterns. He is basically controlling both sides of these conversations. They're not terribly interesting.

An example:

Nic: What a horse with a horn on top?

Me: A horse with a horn on top is called a unicorn.

If I were to say, " A unicorn has a horn and looks like a horse," he would go ballistic. The pattern has to be just right.

Another example:

Nic: How you spell Wolverine? (Famous X-Men character)

Me: W.

Nic: What come after W?

Me: O.

Nic: What come after O?

Me: L.

Nic: What come after L?

Me: V.

And so on. When we get to the last letter he says, " E, E is the last letter in Wolverine?" It's the same with all spelling. The rhythm has to be the same and just right, or he can't spell it.

Nic will talk about the same subjects over and over and over until I'm ready to pull my hair out. Someone at school taught him an intervention for this. So when he's been repeating something just too much, one of us will say, "That's enough sayin' that." Sometimes it stops the repetition. Sometimes it just switches him over to repeating, "That's enough sayin' that" over and over.

He constructs whole complicated sentences, with many names of his action-character friends recast in other settings. I have to say them back in the same order, with whatever the next part of the plotline is. It's like those irritating memory games played at birthday parties when I was a child. I was never good at them.

Example:

Nic: Mamma, Milo is drivin' a excavator.

Me: Oh, Nic, Milo is driving an excavator!

Nic: Kida is drivin' a front-loader and Milo is drivin' a excavator.

Me: Ah, Kida is driving a front-loader and Milo is driving an excavator.

Nic: Mole is drivin' a backhoe, Kida is drivin' a front loader, and Milo is drivin' a excavator.

Me: Oh, Nic, Mole is driving a backhoe, Kida is driving a front-loader, and Milo is driving an excavator. That's about enough sayin' that, Nic.

Nic: No, Momma, just one more time. Vinnie is drivin' a steam-roller, Mole is drivin' a backhoe, Kida is drivin' a front-loader, and Milo is drivin' a excavator.

He usually pushes it beyond "one more time, Momma." He can sometimes get up to six or seven repetitions and my poor memory struggles terribly to repeat them back in the right order with the right names.

The result of these obsessive-compulsive behaviors on the family is that we have a rigid daily routine. There is very little room for spontaneity. This is getting better, but it's still hard. I have friends who toss off comments like, "Hey, we should go to the show sometime." Or, "Let's try that new place for dinner." Or, "You should really go see that play." I would love to do all of those things and more, but if we change the routine too much too fast, Nic falls apart and it takes days to put him back together. They have no idea the price we pay to get out, and that is isolating. We have to do a cost-benefit analysis of every social opportunity that comes our way: *What will we get in terms of entertainment, rejuvenation, and friendship, versus the exhaustion of Nic if he gets too far out of balance when his compulsive routines are disrupted?*

I've had the opportunity to develop patience I never thought possible. Nic's repetitive behaviors are exasperating and highly irrational and seem to be helping him learn something, so I'll keep playing the game. It's not like there's another option.

Disability and Sadness

chapter
8

*S*ometimes life with an autistic child feels like a bottomless pit of sadness. Before we were established in this great classroom, on a bad day at its worst I would feel how isolated Nic was. I'd worry he would never have any friends. One time, Rico, at about age six or seven, burst into tears while we were driving.

"What's up, honey?" I asked.

"Nic will never get married and have kids of his own, will he?"

"No, honey, he probably won't."

Reminders

It's normal to get used to whatever unusual circumstances you live with. That's how the nervous system is designed. If we were aware of all of the stimulation around us all the time, we wouldn't be able to think. As I have adjusted to Nic's disability, it often disappears from the conscious part of my thoughts. It's just how things are at our house. Then something comes along and pulls the rug out from under me. I am still struck by the intensity of the sadness I feel at these times. The grief cycle plays itself out again, and I continue to be surprised. I do it over and over. Every time we hit an easy stretch, I think I've got things figured out and that's how the rest of Nic's life will be. Of course, that's just plain foolish. It's not how life is for the rest of us. Why should it be any different for Nic?

Recently, I gave Rico and some of his friends a ride to the movie theater. Some new friends—who didn't know Nic—got into the van. They weren't used to a kid sitting there shouting at every McDonald's we passed, or to the perseveration that went with much of his speech. They weren't used to ignoring it the way the kids who knew him were. The polite ones catch on that there is something really different about Rico's brother. They keep their eyes open and their mouths shut. The less sensitive try to engage him in a banter that assumes they're on an equal playing field. This banter is often somewhat predatory. On a good day, I use this as a teachable moment. On a bad day, I grind my teeth and think murderous thoughts.

A few months ago I started Nic's morning bath as usual. I left him standing in the bath while I ran to get something in my bedroom. I got distracted while I was there, and it was a few minutes before I got back. Then I heard him quietly calling for me. I ran in and found him "stuck," standing in the bath with the water burning him. Seeing him like this wiped away that veil of illusion that I usually have in place. The veil is there to let me proceed with a normal life. The veil lets me forget how vulnerable he is. But in that moment, I remembered. He was incapable of thinking and then acting to save himself. He should have stepped out of the bath or turned off the water. When he got upset, he lost his ability to ask for help or do the things that most people would do without having to think about it.

Nic is incapable of crossing the road by himself because he can't make a judgment about how far away or fast the cars are.

This is actually a step forward. When he was a preschooler, he didn't comprehend that there was potential danger on the streets. When he was about four, we moved into our new house about two blocks away from our old house. He took off about three times that summer and we nearly lost our minds. We hopped in the car and drove like crazy all over the neighborhood. The neighbors asked if they could help. We felt both embarrassed at being so incompetent as to lose our child and grateful to be surrounded by such well-intentioned people.

We usually found him in a matter of minutes. The longest episode was excruciating. We eventually found him inside the old house, on a chair, getting ice cream out of the freezer. The folks had left the back door unlocked, just as we had when we lived there. They were not home. I don't remember if we ever told them about the missing ice cream or not.

One summer we took a vacation in Baltimore. Honora stayed home with Grandma so she wouldn't miss the start of cheerleading practice for her freshman year in high school. We left the city and drove to the beach, which has always been a relatively soothing place to be. We can always see Nic on a big beach, so we're pretty relaxed about not losing him. He loves all the stimulation of the waves, salt, sand, and sun. The beach is one of those rare places where we all usually have a good time. That day was particularly special. The water was unusually warm and the waves were huge. We played together as a family for hours. After that, we found a restaurant that had unlimited crab legs, and chicken nuggets for Nic. It was a small piece of heaven.

We started the drive back after the sun set. I thought Nic would fall asleep, and that Rafael, Rico, and I then would be able to talk. I anticipated a peaceful end to a perfect day.

Nic started getting agitated. Soon he was in a full-fledged tantrum and we had no clue what it was about. It seemed to come out of nowhere. It went on for more than an hour. He started getting wild, pushing and hitting. I couldn't figure out anything that would help. I sat in the middle seat and tried giving him water to drink, music tapes to distract him, tight holding to help him calm himself, and joint compression. Nothing worked. I was frazzled and he was exhausted. He went to the backseat and sobbed. Then he came up from the backseat and stood in front of me in the moving van and wet his pants. After that he settled down from the anger and just sobbed pitifully. I helped him change into his mildly wet bathing suit, and he eventually fell asleep in the backseat.

I cried in the middle seat. He couldn't tell us that he needed to go to the bathroom.

The Family Package

In day-to-day life, the profoundly impaired ability to communicate is what disables this child. All the sensory weirdness and altered mind function could be coped with if Nic could just tell us what he was experiencing.

The pioneer in me always has to figure out the lay of the land when in new territory. I really like maps. When planning a trip, I read the maps ahead of time. This is a protective mechanism. In case of attack, we will be prepared. I will know a little escape path or where to find water or just where to park my covered wagon. There was no way to prepare for Nic.

Most of us come with an inner sense of the lay of the land, of "how things are." Our parents and families teach this to us. They do it intentionally and unintentionally. The land I was brought up in told me that being smart was really much better than anything else. Working hard was expected from all of us. Dressing nice and having good manners somehow meant you were a good person. That stuff was pretty overt. The covert stuff included such values as "Children were to be seen and not heard," "A wife should be a good homemaker and cook, but never show how much work it takes," and "All a husband had to do is bring in the bucks, and it should be big bucks."

There was nothing unique in this package, and it was fairly common for the fifties. Please know that I intend no disrespect to my parents. My father was, and my mother is, a kind and thoughtful person. American values in the fifties were just as superficial as you would predict with a growing economy and the near-death experience of World War II a decade before.

My husband grew up in the Philippines with a different package. Overt values included becoming classically educated, listening for your vocational calling, and working hard. Unspoken values included being a premier family man, holding God central in a family, and fidelity.

We all have these packages. They serve us for better or for worse. Some people can live their whole lives never examining the package. Some have to rewrite the whole package. Having a child with disabilities will most certainly test the utility of the package.

I remember my father telling stories of great sorrow about families with too many kids, impaired kids, and bad kids. This was a situation to be pitied. The message implied that a really good family wouldn't allow this to happen. Dad was an obstetrician and believed that chromosome sampling and elective termination of genetically defective pregnancies was the ultimate that science could do for humanity. He thought euthanizing an anencephalic baby was an act of kindness. No wonder his denial about his grandson was so extreme.

It is a gentle irony that when my father was quite old, Nic was one of his most comfortable companions. As my father aged, he really only wanted to eat dessert. My mother picked at his nutrition habits in a wifelike way. Dad would drop by the house unannounced and pick up Nic. They would go to the ice cream store and sit in companionable silence, smiling and enjoying their ice cream together, neither fretting after the other about ruining their dinner.

In the fifties, the only answer for a busy professional couple would have been to farm out or institutionalize a child like Nic. When I was growing up, no families in my parents' circle had any kids like this—or so it seemed. As I got older, the secrets were revealed: "So-and-so had a child on a farm out in Bath" or "So-and-so had a child over in Pentwater State Hospital." This was almost always whispered. It was a tragedy too deep to bring out into the light of day. The other secrets were interesting too: who had marriage problems, who drank too much. This closeting of problems made it hard for anyone to express true compassion. We were taught only pity. I have found with secrets that the veneer always comes off. I am thankful to live in more open times.

My husband grew up with what I consider to be a more cosmopolitan view. Kids come in all shapes and sizes, with different abilities. The assignment is to love them as best you can. It is also true that in the Philippines, middle- or upper-class families have enough help to be able to do this with grace. I have often seen this attitude in large Roman Catholic families in my medical practice. I have been warmed and educated by these families.

I have seen large families and small families that flourished, and large families and small families that withered. It seems to me that the predictor of success is flexibility. In a family with lots of surprises, rigid parents don't make it, and they tend to take everyone else down with them. Families without surprises rarely exist.

An inability to solve problems also relates to rigidity. If parents continue to listen to those implied definitions of success and cannot revise them, disaster is in the offing. The downside is this: When you have an impaired child, you have to rewrite the rules. The upside is this: When you have an impaired child, you get to rewrite the rules.

Career Day

When Rico and Honora were in elementary school, they had projects that involved learning about different careers. Often Rafael or I would go into their classrooms and talk about what being a doctor was like. Because of the demographics of our neighborhood, the kids never had electricians or plumbers in to explain the trades. I always thought that was a huge disservice to those little kids. There wasn't a big range of jobs presented, and most of the parents who volunteered were professionals. On a perverse day, I plan Career Day for Nic's class. Dishwasher, grocery-bagger, factory widget-placer—any of these would be a victory for Nic.

No wonder I go off in a huff when I overhear parents in the high school complaining about the inadequacy of the Advanced Placement classes or the lack of language choices for their little mainstream darlings.

Small Joys

I remember sitting at the faculty club pool several years ago. Nic came up to me, excited about a discovery he had made.

"Momma, girls wear dresses, and boys wear pants!"

"Yes, Nic! Girls wear dresses, and boys wear pants."

Our conversations are often fairly loud. When Nic is excited, he has a hard time modulating his voice. He went off to look at something else, and I leaned back in my chair.

A few chairs away I could hear a politically correct young mother saying pointedly to her young daughter, "Girls can wear anything they want to." I could tell by her tone of voice that she was frightened we were spreading sexist propaganda poolside. We probably needed to be enlightened. That mother had the luxury of finding stereotyping offensive.

Nic works so hard at skills that come without effort for other kids. Talk about ego strength. Day after day, he's on a battlefield of sorts, and he just doesn't give up. A mistake I have made is to see what isn't there instead of what is. He can't write effectively, his reading is just beginning, and he can't do any functional math. He does keep working and working, and he continues to grow. The writing and reading he can do amazes me because I never expected him to have any of these skills. His social skills have blossomed and he has lost much of his shyness. Of course, the circumstances need to be just right, but now he enjoys meeting new people, even if the experience is egocentric. (He sees new people as potential additions to his fan club.) In many ways, he works harder than the other kids.

This is a gift from a child like Nic. We have learned to be thankful for the simplest things. All our assumptions were wiped away. In this affluent culture, drenched in media images, material wealth, and general overbusyness, this is a gift. We had the excess scraped off, and I believe our family is closer and more balanced because of it.

The future is a place where many parents of special-needs kids torture themselves regularly. It's easier to give up the illusion of control for a child with a broad array of skills. You figure they'll go out and find their paths all right. They'll make mistakes and have victories, learn some lessons easy and some lessons hard. But it seems like it's almost all hard for Nic.

The future is a morass of potential disasters for a mother with a rich imagination: *Where will he live after we're gone? How do I learn to trust strangers with my vulnerable child?* My optimum picture for Nic is that someday he might live in a home with similarly affected individuals. I'd like it if he could live with his peers. If he can learn to take a bus and do some activity that will earn him a paycheck, however small, it will be cause for celebration.

How do we structure things so he won't be a burden to his sibs? When I think of all the complicated issues young marrieds have to work out regarding the families they come from, it makes me worry for the big kids. On the other hand, Nic's presence in their lives may function as a winnowing fork, helping them to discern the true character of potential mates. We plan and plan, but I really believe we have very little control. The future is something we have learned to give over to God. Otherwise it makes us crazy.

chapter
9

chapter
9 | *Schooling*

How It Used to Be

We did just a little shopping this morning. I'm trying to teach Nic about money. It really comes home to him when shopping for his toys. Toy shopping is one of Nic's major events of the week. He anticipates it for days. He talks about it all week long. We can almost use it as a reward or punishment. Almost. . . .

He got money from his uncle for Christmas. He spent some of it. We counted out the leftover, plus an allowance he didn't blow, plus another allowance. Sometimes he does this with great focus; other times he couldn't care less. Today we picked up a few groceries and spent a lot of time in the toy aisles looking for a toy that wasn't there. He chose a small car instead. I am pleased with how well he handled that disappointment. We were in the checkout line. It was a very slow Monday morning, so everyone was pretty relaxed. It's stupid to go when the place is crowded and tense; Nic just inhales that energy, and it brings out the worst in him. He becomes even slower, more obsessive, and often irritable.

I let him do his transaction before the groceries. I told him what to say to the cashier. "Here, Nic, give her the six dollars."

"Yes, Momma. Here," he said, looking almost directly at the lady. He held out a five and a one that I had given him.

"Now, Nic, she's going to give you back change."

"Thank you," he said in his high, nasal voice. To anyone looking at him and listening, it would have been obvious he's impaired.

She looked right at him and said, "You're welcome!" He smiled and went to sit on the ledge by the window to look at his new car.

"I had a brother who was special," she told me in a soft voice. This was different from what we get a lot of the time. Lots of the time we get tired people who are irritated at slowness. I looked at her. "Where is he now?"

"Oh, he died." She paused in mid-thought. She thought she shouldn't be telling me this. "He committed suicide. It was horrible back then. The kids would taunt and tease . . . it's better now. That was way back in the fifties and sixties when he was coming through. He died when he was twenty-three. It's better for the special ones now." I agree with her. It's better now, and the Americans with Disability Act (ADA) and the public school systems are largely why it's better.

It is a primal parental fear: Someone hurting your child so deeply that the child would find a way to stop his existence. The image of a retarded boy finding a way to self-immolate makes my insides scream.

Later I was out doing errands by myself. I walked by a grown, fat retarded man waiting for a bus. I met his eyes intentionally and gave him a big smile and a hello. He said hello back and his face opened up. He beamed. I wonder how much of a chance he got when he was in school. I wonder where his parents are and what their lives are like now. But mostly I wonder who will be nice to Nic when he is forty-five years old.

Parental Models

My sister, who has no children, said it best: "Well, it seems to me they're like plants. It's the parent's job to figure out how much water and light and what kind of soil they need." Unfortunately, we've all seen family systems that only "do" one kind of crop. There are families that specialize in raising corn, and they do a great job with corn, but all of a sudden it is obvious to the rest of us that they've been given a hothouse orchid.

Oh, my! we think. Some kids recover from this kind of upbringing and are stronger and wiser than we would hope they would have to be. Some people crumple and spend the rest of their lives chasing these emotional issues.

I was talking with my friend Mike at church. He and his wife are an awesome couple. They have opened their house to foster children. They have hoped to adopt, and have one of the three of their foster kids already signed over. The other two are sisters—one a newborn—being dangled in the court system.

Mike and I talked about how parenting perceptions change with time. We talked about how, with the first child, you operate under the illusion that perfection could and should be obtained. The firstborn is catered to and fussed over and worried over. Every detail of parenting is analyzed and debated. If you shout by accident, you're going to have traumatized him for life. If you shout on purpose, this is probably a protective services consult for sure, and should you just turn yourself in? If he has to wait for something or is unhappy, this will surely result in years on a therapist's couch. We talked about how stressful it is for all involved when a firstborn comes into the house.

Mike was holding their fifth child in his arms as we talked. The baby was taking a bottle and staring devotedly into his face. This was their third foster child. We talked about how her older sister had settled down since coming into their home. He remarked about how much a little routine can do for a child. I agree, but I also know that it is delivered with love in their house. He says his expectations now are completely different than before. "You just feed 'em, clean 'em, and love 'em."

He figures they are God's anyway, and they're just passing through his hands momentarily. He'll do the best he can. For control freaks, this is a challenging philosophy to accept.

I believe that parents are much more self-conscious nowadays, and like everything, there is an upside and a downside to this. As for the bad side, we all know parents whose approach is more like they're breeding horses or hybridizing plants. This is the child-as-property model.

"You're my child, and you'll do what I say!"

"No child of mine is going to dress like that!"

"But our people don't do that!"

Whatever! I believe the more accurate model is the biblical idea that parents are stewards. The child is God's, and our assignment is to do the best we can for the spirit in that little human.

I am driven crazy by parents who subscribe to the notion that character can be bought. They think if parents just send their kids to the right school or surround them with the right kind of people or dress them right, then surely they'll fall into some predictable, controlled path that suits the parents' needs.

The good side of this self-consciousness is that many parents try to assess their children's unique needs. They try to offer them enrichment appropriate to their gifts. The downside is that sometimes they pile a whole lot of expectations and busyness onto a kid's life.

I'm probably going to desecrate this story, but I'll tell it anyway. Someone once told me that there is an American Indian belief that when a baby is born, it is the parents' job to call the spirit into that being. The first few months of the baby's life are spent calling to the spirit. If everything is okay after a few months, they go ahead and name the child and then celebrate. It seems a comforting, gentle belief.

With Nic, I feel I have spent years calling to the spirit in him. When he was about three years old, I looked up after wrestling with him to get some poopy diapers changed. He was always wiggly and uncomfortable. Diaper changing of a child this big is no small matter. If you're not talented, the poop goes everywhere, including all over you. They kick their feet, and then it gets on their socks, and then if you don't dodge, it gets on your sleeve, and then when you dodge the other way, it goes from your sleeve to your shirtfront. By then they have got their hands in it, and their overalls are smeared. You get the idea.

My face was all pinched and uptight. I had a flood of realization that this was the face he saw most of the time. I was so tense and anxious when caring for him—trying to anticipate the next disaster—that I never smiled at him. This was a huge revelation to me. I was transported into the seat behind his eyes. All the faces around him, whenever they looked at him, altered. They knit their brows with worry. They were tense and concerned. They were tired and angry.

I got the poop cleaned up and then paused. I looked right at Nic. He looked into my eyes. I grinned at him, a full-fledged sun-in-my-eyes smile. He beamed back at me.

Thereafter, I tried what they call in the books *positive attending*. This is basically being nice to your kid. I tried to spend some time each day nonverbally communicating to him love and approval. I smiled at him a lot more.

Parental Models Go to School

How you think you should behave as a parent and how you think your child should be taught come out of the same deep place inside. Schooling is a very emotional topic. We all know stories of horrible things going on in classrooms, and there is much righteous fodder for the educational reform movement. But rigid thinking about a school's structure erupts from the same dark source as rigid thinking about a successful family.

It gets even more emotional when you throw in disability. With the abandonment of the developmentally disabled by the medical system, the societal responsibility has been shifted to the school systems. A lot of good has come of this. Special services can most conveniently and effectively be served up in this setting. What an experienced special education teacher or occupational therapist or autism specialist has to say about a problem is much more likely to be helpful than what your physician has to say. There is no disputing the advantages to our kids from the ADA and the development of services and accessibility that has resulted from this legislation.

I am always shocked when I run into resentment toward special needs kids and the amount of money spent on their education. I am not aware of people resenting speech rehab services for their elderly stroke relatives or post-closed-head injury rehab for young adults after their skiing, diving, or auto accidents. The public is quite naïve about medical insurance. Many people in my state are so used to extraordinary coverage that they think of their insurance cards like a charge card, with the bill going to someone else. The notion of insurance money being a pooled, collective resource is lost on them.

A more visible form of pooled money is the public-school dollar. This is probably because of the election of local school boards and public voting on school millage issues. Parents feel they have more control over this money and are therefore more vigilant stewards. So they resent the extra dollars it takes to educate disabled kids. They see it as money not being spent on their kids. They are unaware of the shift of this responsibility out of their medical dollar—which they view unrealistically—into the more visible public-school dollar. The idea that these dependent individuals will otherwise end up on welfare, another pooled money pot, is lost on many of them. Basically, the biggest bang for the buck is the money spent on schooling these kids. It will result in less money being spent from the other pots.

The passage of the ADA resulted from years of persistent, effective lobbying by disabled individuals and their families. Part of that early activist movement was the radical notion of inclusion. The concept of least restrictive environment was introduced and determined to be an important goal in meeting the needs of special education students.

This was good. It brought many problems out of the closet. All kids benefit enormously from effective inclusion programs. Both the special-needs child and the typical child benefit, as they do from anything that increases healthy diversity in their classroom.

A few years ago, Cory was part of Nic's special-ed classroom. They spent about two years together. Then it was decided that Cory would do better in a mainstream classroom. He has flourished with the help of a paraprofessional (not a certified teacher, but a person skilled in assisting special-needs students), some great teachers, and a good group of kids. It is tradition in their school at Halloween to parade through all the classrooms. As a visiting parent, I enjoy watching the progression from sweet little five-year-old princesses and fairies to sixth-grade boys pushing the rules as hard as they can, dressed in as bloody and macabre costumes as they think they can get away with. About two years ago, I was in Nic's room, watching the parade. I was pleased to see Cory come parading through, dressed as a muscle man. His foam rubber muscles rippled masculinely and he was clearly enjoying himself. His former classmates stood up and started to chant, "Cory, Cory, Cory." They were so proud of him. It was like the victor had returned. Cory had gone out into the big time and made it. I don't think Rocky could have felt any better.

Ineffective inclusion programs are another matter altogether. When they're bad, everyone loses. But in too many schools, the trend is to push everyone into the mainstream. When that happens, an individual assessment of the child's needs isn't considered, and inclusion is hyped as a goal for all special-needs children.

Nic did not benefit from inclusion. The worst year of his

school career was the year he spent in a mainstream classroom. And this was with the cards stacked in his favor. He had a marvelous teacher, whom he knew from his PPI (pre-primary impaired) classroom. He had a loving and experienced parapro. The parents of the other kids in his class bent over backward to include him. It was simply too much for Nic. There was too much noise, activity, and visual stimulation. All that enrichment was right for the regular kids, but it was toxic for him.

I have two concerns about mainstreaming. The first is what I call malicious mainstreaming. Parents who are still in denial about their child's prognosis commit this. They insist on mainstreaming because they mistake the process of role modeling provided by the other students for a normalizing process. When a year goes by and there is no change in their child, they think the teacher has done something wrong or someone is to blame.

My other concern has to do with the basic nature of humans. My son has known he was different from the get-go. He has communicated this to me in many ways, most of them nonverbal. When you put a child who is profoundly different in with a bunch of fully equipped kids, everyone knows what's going on. If the children have been brought up well, they are polite and practice acts of inclusion as they are able to. Many are very kind. If they have not been brought up well, they can be cruel. Neither of these is an ideal environment because both preclude the development of a real peer group. No one likes to be around kids who've been treated with kid gloves all the time. They tend to be brats. In the opposite direction, any report on school violence will summarize the worst-case effects of taunting, teasing, and other peer cruelty.

I believe a critical mass of time spent with real peers allows true friendships to grow. This is as good as it gets. We found this in Nic's contained classroom.

A good teacher uses these real relationships to teach. Renee, Nic's current teacher, is the gold standard in my book. My son knows about "showing heart" and "giving zingers" because these behaviors are illustrated and discussed in his classroom every day. Renee is able to make these principles concrete.

The continuity we have been blessed with has allowed a real classroom culture to develop. This in turn benefits the younger kids who come into the room. For my son to be a role model for a seven-year-old is huge. He sees himself as competent and feels pride. This is true growth. It helps interrupt the cycle of constant dependence that so many of these kids suffer from. When they're around the regular kids, they are never fast enough or smart enough or acceptable enough. That is an exhausting way to live. If we didn't have a contained classroom, I don't believe these trusting relationships could have developed.

Also, we have a social life. We don't have to apologize for bizarre and irritating behavior at the movies. Birthday parties are as much fun for the parents as the kids because we can talk to people who understand our day-to-day trials.

The children in Nic's class are remarkable. They show pure and simple tolerance of diversity. They are sib-like with each other, which means they can be joyful with each other and then turn around and give each other a hard time. The kid gloves are off, and they're on as even a playing field as they'll ever get. This is a much more balanced environment for them to grow in. Mainstreaming cannot provide this kind of intimacy.

If Nic did not have a brother and sister who gave him grief, wrestled with him, and told him what was cool and what was not, I'd feel the need for some mainstream contact. But he does have these paragons of popular culture in his life, and I am thankful for that.

Nic is "with it" enough now to follow some fads. He may not get the point of the fad, like that you could play a game with Pokemon cards, but he knew the cards were cool and he enjoyed having some because they made him feel cool. Currently, he's obsessed with Harry Potter.

As Nic gets older, the discrepancy between him and his same-age peers becomes more glaring. That's hard. I worry about other children exploiting him when he goes off to middle school. But he has to go to middle school. He's almost the tallest one at his elementary school, and soon he's going to need to shave. I am confident I will survive the transition, and as with every other step he's taken, in addition to the stress, there will be unanticipated victories and treasures.

Nic was finally diagnosed with autism when we had him evaluated at the Autism Center at the University of North Carolina in Chapel Hill. They did a multidisciplinary evaluation over the course of several hours. One of the specialists we saw was a woman who has studied the educational needs of autistic people for more than twenty years. She gave me a wonderful gift. As we were going over the summary of the recommendations they were making, which was all in educational and psychological language I didn't understand, she paused. She looked up, right at me, and said, "Basically, people with autism never stop learning. I've seen people learn to read at eighteen. I've seen people learn to live independently in their thirties. They aren't restricted by these developmental stages like regular learners seem to be."

She opened a door for us. She gave Nic a future. I don't even know if it's accurate, but the notion that Nic will continue to grow and benefit from enrichment changed the way the horizon looks to us. It feels a lot different than the smaller and smaller world we envisioned for him at the worst grip of our fear.

chapter | # Sick
10 | # Nic

Nic came out a big, round, perfect baby boy. He caught on to nursing pretty fast. But he sure was fussy. And he sure didn't sleep. And there sure wasn't much we could do to comfort him. We figured we would just have to tough it out until three months, when most kids settle down from their colic and start to establish a normal sleep pattern.

By six months nothing was much better, and he seemed to throw up a lot. He didn't like to be held. Because he was big, that baby-bucking thing they all do was often a handful.

By the time Nic was nine months old, he was hospitalized with pneumonia, which in retrospect we know was related to his vomiting. But he was gaining weight and length okay and seemed to be developing normally.

He was late to walk, compared to his sibs. He started walking in earnest around fifteen months. Then the language was delayed. Then it was very delayed, and my insides started screaming. I couldn't comfort him. He didn't sleep, he didn't talk, and he threw up all the time. It was hard to distract him. He started to have temper tantrums that were unlike any we had dealt with before. I longed to hold him in my arms while he fell asleep so I could gaze at his beauty. That "sleeping baby in the arms" thing is one of the behaviors kids have built-in to enchant us. They do that to bewitch us and keep us coming back for more. Nic was never able to relax enough for that to happen.

I won't go into detail about the trip to the emergency room when he was two and coughing so hard he could barely breathe. That was when the technician got the diagnosis better than the doctors. I remember more clearly the trip to the ER when he was about three. That was after he ate a bottle of antibiotics. Our neighbor, an intensive care unit pediatrician, calculated he was at the seizure threshold. Rafael gave him the ipecac before we went to the hospital but didn't know it would make him puke (Didn't know it would make him puke? He's a doctor—what did he think we were giving it for?), so he let him jump up and down on the bed until I got there and he could puke on me.

I won't tell you in detail about the time he drank cologne and the poison center said he would get drunk, which he did, with his brother and sister looking on and laughing. I won't tell you in detail about the time he ate mothballs and the poison control center said to watch his urine output because it might wipe out his kidneys. I'll spare you the details of all those stories.

Because of his many seemingly unrelated medical problems, we started with the specialist evaluations. He had ear infections and was language delayed, so was his hearing all right? We had to check it in the hospital with a special test because he couldn't cooperate with the audiologist for even two minutes. The sleepy medicine didn't work right on him. He got hyper instead of sleepy. Then they wanted to try to inject him with something to make him sleepy enough to do the test.

"Mom, will you hold him while we give him this shot?" When they finally were able to administer the test, the answer came back: "Gee, the hearing nerve is working okay; sorry we can't tell you why he's not talking."

"Hey, maybe he doesn't sleep because his reflux is so bad. Maybe we ought to look at his vocal cords." The sedating medicine doesn't work again.

"Mom, will you just hold him down, please, while we finish this procedure that's gagging him and sort of suffocating him too, which we don't want to take the time to adequately anesthetize him for?"

"Will you please hold him down while we stick this wire down his throat to check his esophageal pH?"

"Will you please not go into a rage when the next specialist explains that the first specialist read the test incorrectly and that if you had been here two years ago, we could have helped you then? Will you please keep this child still and prevent him from moving a centimeter while we scan his abdomen with this special test that takes an hour? Will you please get him to settle down while we do his fifth upper GI? Will you please hold him down while we start this IV?"

Finally, the summer he was hospitalized five times, I said I couldn't hold him down anymore. It always made me want to cry and vomit at the same time.

Nic had bouts of severe abdominal pain every six months or so. He would usually drop to the ground and curl up. Then he would vomit and have diarrhea. He actually said, "Momma, take me hospital" when he was about six. I didn't even know he knew the word hospital. To me, it looked like his guts weren't working.

Four hours later he was discharged from the hospital with the diagnosis of constipation. Some subsequent attacks resolved within an hour or so at home. A bad one in April of 1999 went on for too long. Nic asked me to take him to the hospital again. By the time the radiologist came in to do the special gut study, he was better—by then he had fallen in love with the beautiful X-ray technician.

These episodes were awful. He was clearly in severe pain. It was so bad that it was difficult for him to talk, and he certainly couldn't walk. After the April episode, a pediatric surgeon saw him. He scheduled Nic for an exploratory laparotomy in August, when I would have some time off.

In June he resumed vomiting. This time it happened every forty-five minutes through the night. He lay in a puddle of mucus, quietly looking at me while I made all the phone calls to find the pediatric surgeon on call at seven in the morning. The surgeon was different from the one we had seen in the office, but he was a good guy. He made Nic a direct admission to the pediatric floor so we didn't have to go through the nightmare in the ER. Nic continued to vomit, but it was nothing but mucus. He vomited through the X rays, the labs, and the IV start. He vomited through the enema. He was mostly talking to me with his eyes now. He was very frightened. I was too.

Finally they gave him some fancy vomit medicine, and it worked. He stopped vomiting. The stillness was a relief to us both. Then the surgeon came in to examine him. He didn't see the pain and pitiful retching because it was gone by now. He wanted a history, which I gave him as efficiently as I could. It felt like the seriousness of this was going to be lost on him. But then the nurse spoke up. She said something that communicated to the surgeon, in a way I couldn't, that this was really some awful vomiting that had been going on. I am always amazed by how hard it is to communicate the important things.

The results of the physical exam hinted at appendicitis. We watched Nic for twenty-four hours. He was not much better, so the doctor decided to take him to surgery. That was a tremendous relief to me. They found blood in his stomach, an inflamed appendix, and some old scarring around his gallbladder.

The doctor would need to perform an endoscopy to look at Nic's esophagus and stomach to find out about the bleeding, but overall Nic did better after the surgery. He was discharged after the longest four days of my life.

We came back in two weeks for the endoscopy. I told them I couldn't hold him down for anything anymore. The amount of anesthetic they needed to keep him sedated was enough to flatten an elephant. They found his esophagus had torn during the vomiting but was now healing. This is called a Mallory-Weiss tear, and this is not an organ you ever want to tear, because you can't stitch it back up. The gastrointestinal specialist took biopsies. Everyone was sure Nic had reflux so bad that he had chronic inflammation of the esophagus.

Two weeks later he started vomiting again. This put me over the edge. If he started bleeding from the esophageal tear, he could die. The new pediatric surgeon on call for the group made Nic a direct admission again. The intern working with the surgeon wrote an order for an old-fashioned vomit medicine. We went through the trauma of drawing the labs, starting the IV, and getting X rays before they gave him the medicine through the IV.

Everyone left the room, and Nic lay down to rest. I called my mom to tell her we were in the hospital again. All of a sudden he sat bolt upright. His eyes were glowing. He looked right at me and said, "I hate you, Momma." Then he started chewing on his IV site. It made me think of those stories about caged or trapped animals that gnaw off a leg to get free. He was very agitated. Actually, he looked like he was possessed. I called the nurse. She came in and had a very human reaction when under stress: she laughed. This was burned into my heart forever. That simple action, even though I knew it was a stress response, was so inappropriate that I wanted to kill her.

I told her, "I think he is having a drug reaction. In my day, the treatment was IV Benadryl. I don't know if that is what they use now. Please call the intern or attending surgeon right away." She went out of the room.

All of a sudden, Nic flopped down on the bed and his arms flipped up to the side of his head. His head jerked to the side. It was like he was paralyzed in that position. His eyes were terrified. I went out into the hall and hollered something. Suddenly, we had about five people in the room. They were standing all around the bed like they were waiting for him to code. A nurse gave him the IV Benadryl, and slowly the tension and the head-jerking started to lessen. I began breathing again.

This kind of reaction is called a dystonic reaction and it is a known, but fairly rare, side effect of a certain category of medicines.

The pediatric resident said something snotty about how she never used phenothiazines in children. The surgery intern came in hangdog and apologized to me. The attending surgeon never said anything about the whole episode. It was the single most frightening moment of my life with Nic, except for maybe those times when I lost him.

.

chapter 11 | *Losing Nic*

You would think that after the first time, I would have put some system in place to ensure it never happened again— a system like a ball and chain, or an implanted tracking device, à la James Bond. But with time, we tend to forget the intensity of panic associated with our nightmares.

The first time was in the big public park near our home. We were at an annual picnic associated with my husband's work. We enjoyed many of the families who came every year. There were lots of kids and neat playground equipment. The contributed food was all homemade salads and desserts, and the ribs and chicken were catered. In other words, this was the formula for a great time. Nic was about four. He knew very little language, and the language he did use, only his family could understand.

I had a program that was by then built-in to my neurologic system. I think of it as auto-track. Every four to five seconds a small electric spark would go off in my head, requesting the location of Nic. If it sounds uncomfortable, it's because it was. That electric spark seemed also to trigger muscle tension. My husband could tell how bad a day I'd had by how close my shoulders were to my ears. On a good day I had relatively normal posture. On a typical day, I walked around with my shoulders all winched up and my neck stiff, rotating my whole body in order to look in different directions. I've had so much chronic muscle tension that it's taken years of physical therapy, massage, and home exercises to undo the chronic pain. This is a physical consequence of the hypervigilance that is required to raise a child like Nic. It also just plain wears you out. Sleep deprivation makes the intensity of it all worse.

So whenever I tried to have a conversation with someone, it was only halfhearted because so much of my being was monitoring Nic. Mothers of young children are perfectly used to this, and a good friend doesn't even notice if you haven't completed a sentence in four years, because her mind thinks the same way. It is only when you are talking with the conversationally indulged that this becomes an issue. These people actually expect to have a conversation in which people take turns talking and listening and the exchange of ideas occurs. Like the lovely lady I was talking to whose children were grown. She was used to having real conversations with people, and all of her body language, eye contact, and syntax were luring me into a real conversation. I believe it was only for thirty seconds.

I looked up, and Nic was gone. I felt only small panic at first and said, "Excuse me, I have to find Nic. It should take only a few seconds." But the preliminary scanning found no child. My heartbeat increased and I started to sweat. I asked my close girlfriends and their children to help. Soon everyone at the park was looking for Nic. My mind started to spin off into the outer stratosphere, where I observed myself panicking. Someone inside me was struggling to think rationally. Nic didn't like crowds. He had been paying attention to locations and geography lately. *Was it possible he thought he knew how to get home from here? Did he start walking home?* He couldn't cross streets. My worse-case scenario popped up: *He was trying to cross that really big street and was being run over as I stood there.*

My friend John called the police. Two young men came in a cruiser. They were very detached. Actually, they were nervous because the woman—me—who was a basket case was going to lose it completely, and they would have to deal with it. So like many men I know, they adopted a protective layer of detachment to cover their discomfort. (In a marriage, this is the wrong strategy. They can get away with it professionally.) They suggested I sit in the backseat, and they drove me around to see if we could find Nic outside the park. The backseat of the police cruiser was made out of plastic—molded plastic, like the kitchen chairs when I was growing up. It was very uncomfortable. Then I realized they were made that way for easy cleanup after transporting drunk and vomiting college students. We left the park to trace the route home. No Nic. Most of my conscious being was out around the moon by now, looking down on the scene that surely was not reality.

We returned to the park. A crowd had gathered. In the middle were a triumphant Matt and Brad. They had found Nic at the far end of the park where it was fenced in and full of brush and mosquitoes. They were the heroes of the hour. They told me he was just walking around talking to himself, not worried at all.

I got home with all the kids, locked the door, and cried for about an hour. After an event like that, I feel physically sick. The science-fiction thinker in me wonders about the sense of detachment, that out-in-the-stratosphere feeling. Is the sickness the result of the spirit reinhabiting the body? Is that what it's going to feel like when I die? I also think it's because about two years of life span was scraped off my nervous system.

The next time was worse. We were in Baltimore at a conference for my husband. We stayed right there on the waterfront at a wonderful development: comfortable hotel, great restaurants, a children's museum, and the National Aquarium.

We wandered through the aquarium on our second day there. It was a success. Nic was interested in all the fish, and the dark lights and quiet were very soothing for such a big public space. It was packed. We finished up our tour and went to the gift shop, which was full of a swarm of kids on a field trip. It was *really* packed. Nic and I were feeling claustrophobic. We cruised the aisles until we found some reasonable treasures. The crowd was thinning, but Nic hates that closed-in feeling, so I asked Rico to go with him out the exit and wait for me right there while I stood in the checkout line to make our purchases. I finally got through the line and went out.

They weren't there. I thought I'd told them to stand right outside the exit. Then I thought maybe Nic got antsy, so Rico took him to walk around. I looked around. The plaza was enormous. It was filled with groups of people. It was exactly where a sociopath pedophile would come to steal a child. I certainly was glad I appreciated that detail early in the escapade. I willed myself to be patient and not panic.

Perhaps they had just gone to the bathroom. *Oh, God! That's even worse.* The thought of those two beautiful boys alone in a public restroom made me start to feel nauseous. I again willed myself not to lose it. The boys were eight and ten and had golden skin, pink cheeks, brown Filipino eyes, and bowl haircuts. They were luscious.

I don't remember where or when I lost the will not to panic. The sea of hysteria opened up before me, and I jumped right in. *I will never be able to recover from this. I will end up killing myself if anything has happened to them,* I thought. I envisioned my hysterical, raving face on the evening news, begging for the return of my sons. I could see the FBI men coming to interview me, checking me out to see if I was guilty. "Now Mrs. Javier, just how difficult was your son?" I was over the edge.

My last lifeline was the possibility that Rico, who always has a key for the hotel, had decided to take Nic back on his own. I left the square, tears streaming and chest squeezing so hard I could barely breathe. I went up to the room. I could hear the silence from the end of the hall. No kids. I went to my husband's meeting room and charged in, right in front of fifty people, and grabbed him. I waited until we got out of the room before I started bawling. He called hotel security. They told us to go back to where we lost the children and inquire at security there. They would call the harbor police. Those words felt like a death sentence to me.

Rafael took the sobbing, hysterical heap of his wife by the hand and led me across the street to the entrance to the aquarium, where we were directed to security.

Yes! They had two lost boys. Could we describe them please? The big uniformed black woman asked us to wait just a moment.

"It's gonna be all right, honey. Those boys are just fine. My partner has 'em over in the break room. It'll just take a second to get 'em over here. It's gonna be all right, honey." She patted my hand. I wondered if I could go home with her and curl up on her lap. She was very comforting.

When the boys appeared from behind some big metal "don't-come-through-here door," they had a look of excitement, not terror, on their faces. It certainly had been invigorating for them to be lost. They got Cokes and crayons.

Later Rico told me, "Ma, the lady said for us not to be upset when we saw you and that you were really losing it. Are you mad?" His side of the story was that he wasn't comfortable going outside, so he thought they would just stand by the door and wait. Somehow I got by them without his seeing me. "No, honey, I'm not mad. Crazy, but not mad."

The most recent losing-Nic story had some real firepower to it. Firepower in terms of men in uniforms, guns, and police paraphernalia.

Nic continues to mature in ways we never anticipated. He has real attachments to many people. In the fall after Honora went to college at N.Y.U., we saw an abrupt change in some of his behavior. He had made it clear while she was packing, and generally keeping the household in upheaval, that the " move" word would not be used. We were allowed to say she was "visiting" college.

This kept him tantrum-free until September 11, 2001. All that day, I sat in front of the TV with my map of New York City on my lap. It took Honora six hours before she could get a line through to tell us she was okay. By that time, I had determined the distance between her dorm and the World Trade Center was 1.2 miles. We were all agitated. Nic came home that day to very uptight vibes. He reads vibes, often before we know what's going on. We tried to explain to him as simply as we could why we were upset: Some bad men had driven an airplane into some buildings, people had died, and lots of people were sad and worried. We were particularly worried because his Nor-Nor was very close to this bad thing.

Soon he started acting out. First at school, then at home, all these little mini-tantrums started up. For the first time in his life, he was mean and mouthy to his teacher. He actually scratched her, saying he wanted to see her blood. This was shocking to us. Thankfully, she is incredibly professional and very loving. She just wanted to figure out what was up with him.

I also was perplexed. I asked my doc girlfriends. I asked the psychiatrist. I asked the school autism specialist. I asked the church girlfriends. Over the next few days, the answers came back uniformly that he must be upset about Honora.

Why didn't I see that? Wanda the autism guru went over Autism 101 with me, again. "Make it concrete for him, Mary. Get Nora's picture out. Get the map out to show him where she is. Get the calendar out to show him when he'll see her next."

After school that day, Nic got off the bus and came in for his snack. I had the stuff ready. He glanced at Nora's picture and then looked me straight in the eye. "Duh she still love us?" There, it was out. It was as simple as that. The tension fizzled out of the room. "Yes, honey, she loves you very much." His posture improved. He settled down. The next time Honora called, he was even willing to talk to her for ten seconds, which I had been unable to get him to do before. Things straightened out at school. There were no more bad words or scratching the teacher to see blood.

Then he started to focus on the beloved babysitter Neely. He wanted to walk by her house every time we were out on a stroll. He wanted to drive by her house every time we were in the car. Oh, boy—I had my own little stalker. Fortunately, Neely is good-humored and handled this with directness and composure.

One evening, Rafael and I went out to dinner. We don't seem to get out often. The food and company were outstanding. I relaxed more than I had in weeks. That should have been my tip-off.

Neely gave the boys supper. She cleaned up, got Nic his bath, gave him his sleepy medicine, and read to him. At this time, he had been sleeping out on the porch on an air mattress. He's always floated around with his sleeping places, like next to our bed, under our bed, on the floor in the hall, and occasionally in his bunk bed. Sleeping on the porch lasted the longest. I think he liked the sound of the birds, the cool in the summer, all the fresh air, and the stars. I do too. Neely finished his book, kissed him good night, and left as previously arranged. Rico was watching TV in the room that goes out onto the porch. At 9:45, Nic asked for a drink of water. Rico gave it to him and kissed him good night again. We came home at about 10:15. I went upstairs to change my clothes, and Rafael went out to the porch to kiss Nic good night. He came to the bottom of the stairs and shouted up to me, "Mary, where's Nic?"

"Downstairs on the porch."

"No, he's not." Now he had my attention. We both grilled poor Rico. Then we looked through the house. I started to go nuts. I was afraid he had decided to walk to Neely's. Rafael and Rico checked the house from the attic to the basement, including Nora's room and all the closets. No Nic. Still in my nightgown, I got in the car and started driving all over the neighborhood like a crazy woman. I went over to Neely's. No Nic. This wasn't making any sense to me. He had been so comfortable lately. He never crossed streets without permission. Most of this upset was in my head. It hadn't made it to my chest or stomach yet. I drove back home. Rafael was on the phone to the police department. They suggested we minimize traffic on the porch so we wouldn't ruin the scent for the tracker dog they were going to get. They also requested we minimize traffic in the yard. We had checked the front and back yards when this all started.

Soon two police officers arrived. They looked about sixteen years old. They were very calm. They asked all the right questions. One of them had a walkie-talkie on his shoulder that kept sputtering as he talked back and forth on it in police language. They explained that the dog from the state police would be here soon. The doorbell rang, and there was another sixteen-year-old with a gorgeous German shepherd named Alex. It is startling to find one's panicked geezer-self in such youthful hands. It's even more startling when you realize they are very competent hands.

The distress entered my chest. It hadn't arrived at my heart or stomach yet. We explained to the officer about the recent bout of acting-out behavior. "But we thought he was over that." My stomach kicked in when we found the door from the porch to the outside unlocked. It is always locked.

Two of the officers and the dog went out to the porch. We hadn't been out there since they advised us not to "contaminate the scene" (those words gave me the willies). We heard them go out the door, and then I was really about to lose it. My heart was getting involved.

In thirty-two seconds, an officer's walkie-talkie went off: "We found him!"

Nic was outside under the pine tree in the side yard. He had taken his bedclothes out and was under the stars on the balmiest night in weeks. He looked up groggy from the cozy nest he had made and was thrilled to have Alex the police dog licking his face. He has always loved a person in uniform, and here were three tall, handsome men with lots of equipment on paying attention to him.

He was, of course, unable to explain to us why he did this. The weather, stars, and fresh air explained it to me. I think the planets were calling to him in an energy he feels more strongly than the rest of us do.

A few minutes later, there were three more officers stomping their feet on the front porch and asking if everything was okay. The lead officer had these other three out searching the neighborhood without us knowing. They told me they always go to the parks and any construction sites first. I guess they've done this before. That's exactly where Nic would have been if he could cross streets. So the upside is that he had an adventure. The downside is it took about three more years off my nervous system. We still talk about Alex the wonder dog.

chapter | *Destructive*
12 | *Nic*

How I could get to the end of this book and almost forget to include this chapter is a testament to denial. I have become so used to the sense of impending material disaster that I no longer recognize it as a force in the house. Also, it is so much better than it used to be that I really am much more relaxed. Most of the time.

I don't believe any of Nic's incredibly destructive actions have been malicious. This energy just surrounds him, the way dust particles circle around Pig Pen in *Peanuts*. He has now developed so much internal language and sense of self that he is very quick to remind anyone within hearing distance that it was "Jus an accident, Momma, jus an accident. I'm a good boy, right, Momma?"

"Yes, Nic, you're a good boy. It was just an accident."

But Nic does have a tendency to wreak havoc, and it correlates with his hyperactivity. When his medicines are on board, he has much better impulse control. This morning he was running from the bathroom, buck naked, into his bedroom to get his clothes. He found Jane, who helps keep the house clean, in there cleaning. He now has such an appropriate sense of self that he is not comfortable being naked around strangers. (YES! Growth does happen.) Surprised, he backed off and grabbed a dust mop that was leaning against the doorpost. His anxiety expressed itself as energy in his hands, and before we knew it, he had twisted the handle off the mop end. He broke the plastic fitting right off. This was penny-ante destruction compared to when he was younger.

He seemed to have an almost magnetic attraction to any of his brother's new toys. There were many years when Rico went to bed sobbing at the end of his birthday. Nic always seemed to know which present Rico liked the best and went for it. He could break it or lose an essential piece within hours. I find it admirable that Rico has never once tried to kill him.

For years, anything with a screw on it piqued Nic's interest. For being fine motor impaired, he has been able to disassemble some remarkably complex objects. His sister's wicker daybed comes to mind. The other interesting detail was that he did this almost systematically. He worked on all the screws and got them just to the point where all it took was one fatal bounce and the whole bed caved in.

The chairs and stools he has taken apart pale in comparison to the bed. He never actually got a chair to collapse on one of us, though he came pretty close a few times.

He has known not to go near any lawn equipment that's running. I think the noise repels him. But that doesn't hold true when these remarkable objects are turned off. On more than one occasion we have gone out to the garage to get the snowblower, lawn mower, or leaf blower and grabbed it, only to have the handle come off in our hands. He has also gone after his own stuff in the garage. The tricycle, the road racer go-cart thingy, and the large toy excavator that he could actually sit in were all disassembled in their time.

For a while we had to leave pliers by all the lamps because Nic would take the switch knobs off as fast as we could replace them.

When he was quite young, he could enter a room unfamiliar to him and find the most dangerous or fragile object in the room within thirty seconds. We always wondered if he could somehow make a living off this remarkable skill. My father wanted to give Nic fifty bucks for finding Grandpa's hearing aid jammed down into the chair cushions. Usually he would find things like knives or scissors.

If he found himself in a relatively benign room, he could be creative in evoking disaster. Not finding any paper, he went for Grandma's newly recovered chairs with his indelible markers. He has also displayed remarkably sophisticated taste, like the 150-year-old Japanese plate someone left within his reach. My father had a good time gluing the fifty-something pieces back together. He good-heartedly said it was like a jigsaw puzzle.

Toilet flushing has become its own genre. We have paid money to have underwear, pajamas, X-Men, socks, stuffed animals, and numerous McDonald's toys scooped out of the plumbing. These things often snowball. One time when the toilet stool actually had to be lifted, the porcelain in the fifty-year-old stool cracked, which forced the purchase of a new stool and gasket. So we got the new sink, and while we were at it, we had the old flooring replaced too.

My personal favorite was when Nic acted on an urge I had been suppressing for years. I walked upstairs after hearing Rafael rumbling around frantically. I walked into the bedroom and found him with a towel wrapped around his naked body. He was trying to dry off his pager. Nic had intentionally dropped it in the toilet while his father was in the bathtub, looking on. Rafael was unable to resuscitate the instrument and had to go beeperless the rest of the day, as the company programmed a brand-new high-tech pager for him. Interestingly, they couldn't locate the cheaper low-tech version to replace it with.

One summer, the window screens fascinated Nic. We found him systematically poking holes through the screens with a pencil one evening. We tried to explain that this wasn't okay. I tried to give him some old screen from the basement to poke. It just didn't have the same appeal. He did try to cooperate, however. A week later when I found him at the screens, he was using a pair of scissors, not a pencil anymore.

The ultimate disaster was the 150-year-old, seven-foot gilt pier glass mirror that my mother's cousin had given me. This was the same generous lady that gave us the Japanese plate. The glass weighed about 150 pounds. It took two strong men to hang it on my bedroom wall. It was beautiful.

I walked into the house after a long day at work. (They were all long days at work. Even a half-day had a way of becoming a long day.) The babysitter was sitting in the kitchen, looking peaked.

She said, "You're going to be really upset when you go upstairs. But everybody is safe." She looked back down at the ground.

I walked by the TV room. Nora looked up. "Ma, you're going to be really upset when you go upstairs, but everybody is okay."

I found Rico in the living room, playing with Legos. "Momma, you're going to be real upset when you go upstairs, but don't worry. Nic is just fine."

I was ready for anything by now. Nic was nowhere in sight. I climbed up the stairs and walked into my bedroom. The entire room was covered in glass shards and pieces of gilt. The bulk of the frame was torqued into a parallelogram, wrapped around the foot of my bed. I was furious. The rage soared and then it took a turn. The desire to kill Nic transformed to relief that the mirror had not killed him. I was thankful to have the rage whimper away softly.

It took two hours to clean up the mess. I later gave the gilt pieces to an artist. I wanted something good to come out of the disaster. She felt like it was a gold mine. It actually was. Nothing is made out of that quality of gilt anymore.

While cleaning up, I obtained numerous cuts. This mirror was made way before safety glass was a glimmer in anyone's eye. In the edge of the frame, behind the glass, I found a note. It was dated November 17, 1848. It was written in beautiful script with a pencil: "Cold November day, partly sunny. We will drive over to Spring Arbor this afternoon after we finish this job." It sent shivers up my spine. I felt like some cosmic loop had been completed as I read this message that was hidden in the mirror almost exactly 150 years to the day. The date I found the note was November 11, 1998. Maybe some ghost could rest in peace now. I was really scrounging around to find some good in this disaster.

Nic had been entertaining himself by rocking the mirror back and forth against the wall. The babysitter got to him just as the mirror was starting to fall. Why he wasn't injured is not a mystery to me. I have always felt he had some little bubble of God-protection around him. He's just had too many times when something should have happened but hasn't.

chapter | *Economics*
13

W hat we have done with our children with developmental disabilities is scandalous. We have tossed them out of the medical model altogether.

Most insurance companies specifically exclude problems related to autism, retardation, or Pervasive Developmental Disorder. We have made this the responsibility of the school systems. Speech therapy, physical therapy, adaptive anything goes through occupational therapy, all of which falls under the school system. This has the advantage of providing a holistic approach in one dominant environment of these children.

However, the degree of subspecialist expertise many of these kids have access to is severely limited. Many insurance companies will not pay psychiatrist charges for medication management or behavior management if one is so naïve as to use the correct diagnosis for billing. You have to use symptom names, like insomnia or sleep disorder, to get this stuff covered. The help with behavior management needed by most of these kids is well beyond the abilities of the average school psychologist. Few insurance policies will cover state-of-the-art care in this area.

Compare this with how we treat adults. A fifty-year-old male who has smoked all his life, is obese, never exercises, and is oblivious to his diet and lifestyle can have a heart attack and get fifty thousand dollars of medical care thrown at him in less than forty-eight hours. We will then send him back out into the world, after his bypass, with no requirement that he change the habits that have been clearly proven to contribute to his illness.

This reflects our commitment to honor his independence. It denies the interconnectedness of humans, of which an insurance company is a dramatic institutional example. Now this guy can go back out and do it all again, and we'll pay the second fifty thousand dollars as glibly as we paid the first.

These are all choices this man is allowed to make. My child did not make any choice about his disability. He did not choose to live with a neurologic system that is scrambled. He needs help, lots of help. When he was two years old, no one threw fifty thousand dollars at him to help him get started on a healing path. We were nickel-and-dimed every step of the way by an uncoordinated, inadequately funded and resourced set of institutions. The poor school system is always looking over its shoulder at who's coming at it with regulation and lawsuits. Ironically, the school system (not the medical system) is where you will find the experts in managing these disorders, but the bureaucratic regulation and financial realities they are encumbered with often tie their hands about doing the right thing for these kids.

When you look at the decreasing value of the healthcare dollar, you understand why our government and insurance companies are beginning to pay attention to the fine points of preventive medicine. It has finally dawned on them that prevention and impeccable chronic disease management lower total health costs. This is not glamorous work. It's slow, painstaking work. It is what the school systems are doing for these kids. The money spent in the school system is money not being spent in the medical system and will ultimately save money in the welfare system. The long-term care needs of this population are going to be staggering. It is very important that we do everything we can to maximize these kids' potential. That means early, aggressive intervention.

I believe that part of this economic conflict is a result of the very human tendency of denial. When the problem is an invisible disability, it's easy to minimize all that may be at stake. This denial is not in our individual or societal best interest. The research that has been done in this area supports the benefit of early, aggressive, multidisciplinary interventions. However, I hasten to add that the research is challenging to evaluate and the economics are baffling. How does one design a controlled study to evaluate interventions for a lifetime disability? How does one perform a cost-benefit analysis of a disabled individual's life? I believe it ultimately comes down to our values as a secular society, and this makes me very nervous.

chapter	*What I've*
14	*Learned*

As he went along, he saw a man blind from birth.
His disciples asked him, "Rabbi, who sinned, this
man or his parents, that he was born blind?"
"Neither this man nor his parents sinned," said
Jesus, "but this happened so that the work of God
might be displayed in his life." (John 9:1-3, NIV)

*T*his passage states so succinctly a human pattern we still see today. People feel a powerful need to pass judgment. They think that when bad things happen, there must be some cause and effect. Someone must be at fault. This ties in to the illusion of control so rampant in society today. If God punishes people when they screw up, then we can control our lives and avoid disaster by following an external set of prescribed rules. Biblical scholars refer to this as "legalism." Christ's answer suggests that this outlook is warped, and it is part of why he was such a revolutionary.

I have searched for God's hand in Nic's life. One thing I see: The transformation that living with Nic has produced in my life and our family is a miracle. He has allowed us to experience as unconditional a love as is humanly possible. I see the problems of leisure, affluence, and assumptions that so many families suffer from, and I know we have been spared that. We have been forced to declare our priorities and dump everything else overboard. Ultimately, that is a very freeing process.

Before we could come to this point, though, we had to wade though years of chronic grief. It has only been through acknowledging that process and going though it, not around it, that I believe we could come to this place of grace.

Another glimpse of God: The person Nic is becoming fascinates me. He has pure curiosity. His brother loves to dip cookies in milk. Nic looks to me for a point of etiquette on this curious planet, wondering if he may dip his cookies into the water in front of him. He asks interesting questions: "Momma, do we eat stuffed animals?" "Momma, can we dress Serena [the dog] up like a bunny? Can we make a rabbit suit for her?"

His innocence is a balm to a world-weary soul. The most manipulative plot he is capable of is maneuvering me into the toy aisle at Meijers. The foulest language he can come up with is "piggy poop" and "stinky butt."

He is invested in the game of life and desperately wants to please us. He works diligently at school with a focus that exceeds what I was capable of at the most intense period of my medical training. His sight-reading vocabulary is mushrooming. His math skills surpass anything I expected of him. The growth of his language is dazzling. The complexity of his sentence structure and new words surprises me daily. His articulation is steadily improving. On our walk yesterday, he showed me the concept of left and right. He told me to put the dog's leash in my left hand, not my right. It was like he was waiting for an opportunity to show off this new knowledge.

His sleep is deep most of the time. Our sleep has normalized enough to survive the occasional disruption. He lets us cuddle him at bedtime. He frequently asks us to "snuggle" him. This tenderness fills me with feelings of love. We are making up for all the years he couldn't tolerate our touch and it was so hard to console him.

His tantrums have decreased in frequency and intensity. His compulsions are less disruptive. They are more like fascinating eccentricities now. I have thirteen transformer vehicles lined up on my dresser right now. They've been there for a month. Nic's just not sure where he wants to put them yet. Also, I think he likes to keep a stake in our room. It gives him some kind of security.

He wears normal clothes all the time now. His sister and brother are no longer embarrassed to be out in public with him. In fact, he's quite handsome. I'm contemplating selling him to *GQ* as a model.

He sits in the car in the backseat with his seat belt on always. He eats a wide variety of foods. If you get to him while he's hungry and put fruits and vegetables in front of him, he will wolf them down indiscriminately.

In short, he is a miracle. In the last few months, when he's feeling great, he says, "I feel a song comin' on." Then he squeakily hums a few sweet bars of whatever they're working on in school. When he was sick at school a few weeks ago, he told his teacher, "I've lost my song."

I've thought about this story for a long time. It's been my life for twelve years. I am at a phase now where I feel I'm on a path out of these particular woods. During the most horrible parts of those years, the isolation was the worst of it for me. The combination of problems we were dealing with exquisitely depleted us of our coping abilities. I didn't have the equipment to deal with so many problems all at once. We struggled and struggled. When I look back at where help came from, I see it as one tiny step at a time. Eventually the tiny changes merged into a trend, and finally we have found our family in a sailboat going in a direction we never anticipated, with a pretty brisk wind at our backs. It is often exhilarating.

The growth, beauty, and simplicity Nic has brought to our lives bring me joy every day. The amazing people we have met who devote their work lives to the education and care of disabled individuals have cured me of a cynical worldview.

Rafael is always looking for savant capability in Nic. He hasn't found it yet. I think the Gift of Nic is his effect on the world around him. Watching him grow is like an Easter egg hunt with bright-colored jewels around every corner. I look forward to the future with joyful anticipation of the surprises it will hold.

About the Author

MARY SHARP, M.D., completed her medical training in family practice in 1984. Her practice was in traditional family medicine until she took a sabbatical in 2001. In the fall of 2002, she returned to medicine to provide primary care services to kidney patients in a limited capacity.

She married Rafael Javier, a kidney doctor, in 1985. They live in East Lansing, Michigan, and have three children: Honora, Richard, and John Dominic. She believes God has used her family and patients to teach her most of what she has learned about life.

Mary enjoys travel, gardening, and uninterrupted sleep.

MORE GREAT RESOURCES FROM PIÑON PRESS.

Parenting with Love and Logic

Parents have only a few years to prepare their children for a world that requires responsibility and maturity for survival. This book helps parents raise healthy, responsible kids.

by Foster Cline, M.D. and Jim Fay
0-89109-311-7

365 Ways to Help Your Child Learn and Achieve

In addition to being creative, simple, and fun, these ideas are carefully designed to promote positive attitudes about learning, improve memory, encourage creativity and new interests, strengthen your parent-child relationship, and more!

by Cheri Fuller
0-89109-854-2

Angry with God

Beneath anger, frustration, fear, or depression often lies a silent struggle with faith. But what do you do when you're angry with God? Here's help for working through these emotions in your faith journey.

by Michele Novotni, Ph.D. and Randy Petersen
1-57683-222-8

To get your copies, visit your local bookstore, call 1-800-366-7788, or log on to www.pinon.org. Ask for a FREE catalog of Piñon Press products. Offer #BPA.